Writing about Literature

Writing about Literature combines detailed practical and scholarly advice with a sense of the scope and creative possibilities of literary criticism, empowering the student reader to make his or her own discoveries and experiments with language. In addition, it gives valuable guidance on adult language learning and translation skills for students of foreign literature.

This handy, accessible guide covers all aspects of the essay-writing process, including:

* preliminary reading, and choosing and researching a topic;
* referencing and presentation;
* computer use;
* the art and craft of writing;
* style, structure, vocabulary, grammar and spelling;
* scholarly and personal insights into the problems and pleasures of writing about literature.

Writing about Literature is designed to help its readers do exactly that. Written in an entertaining and informative way, and containing a wealth of practical advice and scholarly insights, this wise, witty and helpful book should be on every literature student's bookshelf.

Judith Woolf is a Senior Lecturer at the University of York, where she teaches English and Italian literature.

Writing about Literature

Essay and translation skills for university students of English and foreign literature

Judith Woolf

Routledge
Taylor & Francis Group

LONDON AND NEW YORK

First published 2005 by Routledge
2 Park Square, Milton Park, Abingdon, Oxon, OX14 4RN

Simultaneously published in the USA and Canada
by Routledge
270 Madison Ave, New York, NY10016

Routledge is an imprint of the Taylor & Francis Group

© 2005 Judith Woolf

Typeset in 10.5/12pt Bembo by Graphicraft Limited, Hong Kong
Printed and bound in Great Britain by TJ International Ltd, Padstow, Cornwall

British Library Cataloguing in Publication Data
A catalogue record for this book is available from the British Library

Library of Congress Cataloging in Publication Data
A catalog record has been requested for this book

ISBN 0-415-31444-5 (hbk)
ISBN 0-415-31445-3 (pbk)

In loving memory of
ROBIN HOOD

Contents

Preface

I am extremely grateful to Katrina Attwood for her support, encouragement, chivvying and technical advice, and for co-authoring the section on 'Using Google'; to Karen Hodder for her help with literary theory; and to Anna Clarkson and Philip Mudd at Routledge for their patience and hard work. My greatest debt is to all the students whose struggles and triumphs have been both the inspiration and the source material for this book.

I had hoped to be able to thank Robin Hood for casting his wise and critical eye over the manuscript, but his sudden death in January 2004 has left me instead with the far harder task of thanking him for thirty years of friendship. Robin had a rare ability to guide students into making their own discoveries, and his sharp eye for textual detail and slow, considered delivery of shrewd observations, unexpected insights, and stories with a twist made teaching with him an education and a delight. No university teacher since Alcuin has ever put more scrupulous and painstaking care into helping his students improve their written work, and the same care and practical kindness went into counselling students in difficulties or distress.

Friendship with Robin was a form of cultural exchange in which we invariably remained in his debt. But for him we would never have heard the voices of Henry Irving and Ellen Terry, or the Gaelic psalm-singing of Murdina and Effie MacDonald, or noticed that, in Joseph Strick's film of *Ulysses*, Joyce's 'packet of Epps's soluble cocoa' has been replaced by Fry's. Robin was larger than life, and life seems smaller to us without him.

Most great teachers are fated to leave their best memorial in the minds of former students who have long ago forgotten their names.

It is not only for the obvious reason that that could never be true of Robin Hood.

Quiet consummation have,
And renowned be thy grave!

Chapter 1

Introduction

> To know the road ahead, ask those coming back.
>
> (Chinese proverb)

Conventional study guides and essay-writing manuals can be positively unhelpful to literature students, since the kind of advice about researching and structuring an essay which is useful and relevant if you are studying history or sociology or law is only too likely to prove limitingly rigid and restrictive when applied to such a creative and wide-ranging subject as literature. This book has been written especially for university students of English and foreign literature and tries to combine detailed practical advice with an introduction to the intellectual scope and imaginative possibilities of literary criticism. It covers every stage of the essay-writing process, from reading the text and choosing and researching a topic to referencing and presentation, as well as giving advice on safe computer use and tackling the all-important question of will-power. For students of foreign literature there is also a section on adult language learning and translation skills. However, the major emphasis throughout is on the art and craft of writing. If you have an ambition to write as well as possible about literature, both because it is a subject you are passionately interested in and because you are eager to make your own discoveries and experiments with language, this book is for you.

If, on the other hand, you have chosen to study literature at university because you are passionately interested in student politics or journalism or sport, or because you want to take a degree in the subject you came top in at school as a prelude to becoming a librarian, accountant or lawyer – all good and honourable reasons for taking a degree in literature – then this book will give you a useful grounding in the technicalities of structure, vocabulary, grammar, punctuation and spelling, as well as helping you with background research, computer skills and presentation, but it won't pretend to tell you how to get a decent degree result without the expenditure of anything much in the way of time, patience and hard work. This is a guidebook, not a primer. It doesn't dictate how you should interpret the literature you write about or steer you towards one particular school of criticism, it doesn't give you model answers or pre-packaged ways of constructing an essay, and it certainly doesn't offer you neat formulae for impressing your tutors or bluffing your way through exams. Instead it tries to help you to think through your own ideas and express them cogently and lucidly. In other words, this is primarily a book for people who want to learn a challenging professional skill, and are prepared to put in the hours, and the effort, and the independent thought needed to become real writers.

No one ever writes a handbook for aspiring writers without having a political agenda, whether overt or buried. When the radical and activist William Cobbett published his *Grammar of the English Language* in 1823, he declared on the title page that it was 'Intended . . . especially for the Use of Soldiers, Sailors, Apprentices, and Plough-boys'. His book was explicitly written to empower its disenfranchised readers by enabling them to play an articulate and forceful part in political protest, and thus 'to assert with effect the rights and liberties' of their country, for 'tyranny has no enemy so formidable as the pen'.[1] My own book is the result of thirty years of teaching English and Italian literature in the changing climate of British university education. It is written in the belief that the study of literature, far from being an elitist glass bead game or a sophisticated means of grading young people for their place in the labour market, is a vital interpretative process which enables us, as no other discipline can, to put together the disparate and contradictory and difficult stuff which makes us human. No complex culture can survive for long if it loses touch with that humanity, so serious literary critics also help to assert the 'rights and liberties' of us all. However, the real purpose of the enterprise can only too easily be forgotten in the face of ever-growing public concern with test results and grades, targets and mission statements. If teachers go on wanting to teach despite this, it is because their students still approach literature with fresh and personal excitement and still wrestle ambitiously with the problems of self-expression.

In a culture so preoccupied with testing and grading, it can be hard even for bright and committed students not to feel that their tutors − or the author of a book such as this one − are being remiss if they fail to pass on the great secret of how to get top marks for essays and exam scripts, but the truth is that, in a creative subject such as literature, the only way of ensuring that you score the highest possible marks for your essay is to stop worrying about the marks and concentrate on making as good a job as you can of the essay. This is also the only way − in a society in which the teaching of literature can sometimes seem like an ingenious means of making young people conform to a set of cultural norms − to ensure that your writing will empower you by enabling you to discover and find words for what you really want to say.

This book does not set out to instruct you how to write, but rather to help you to discover how to teach yourself, as professional writers, great and small, have always had to do. The most important message it aims to convey is the one which William Cobbett directed to the soldiers, sailors, apprentices and plough-boys for whom he wrote his *English Grammar*, and to the fourteen-year-old son to whom he affectionately addressed it. As a sharp-minded political thinker, Cobbett firmly believed that there were only two reasons why someone would write something in a less than lucid way: either because they were unable to focus their thoughts sufficiently to communicate them clearly or because they were trying to sell some-one snake oil. What is true of political writing is true also of literary criticism. However complex or sophisticated the ideas you want to put across, wilful obscurity will never enhance them, nor will any discerning reader think that they are more intelligent or striking for being unnecessarily opaque. In fact, the serious creative and critical effort you need to put into making them clear will enable you to test out their validity. As Cobbett told his son James (and the italics are his): '*Never write about any matter that you do not well understand. If you clearly understand all about your matter, you will never want thoughts, and thoughts instantly become words.*'[2] That 'instantly' may cause you a wry smile as you draft and redraft your opening paragraph, but otherwise this is invaluable advice.

Advice is what the middle-aged have always offered the young: measure twice and cut once; *i* before *e* except after *c*; walk three times round yonder church and never think on a fox's tail.[3] Writing this essay-writer's guide, I have sometimes felt like a Jewish mother standing on the quayside as my readers embark on the great voyage of life and calling, 'Always back up your work and don't forget your stapler.' All teachers spend their professional lives on that quayside, since the end and aim of all teaching is the day when the teacher is no longer needed; so I should like to end this Introduction with the words of another powerful social critic who, like Cobbett, wrote an *English Grammar*: the dramatist and poet Ben Jonson. (He was a contemporary of Shakespeare, so forgive him the gender-specific language.) If there is indeed a secret to the production of successful interpretative prose, then this one sentence contains it. Achieve this and you can call yourself a writer.

> A man should so deliver himself to the nature of the subject, whereof he speaks, that his hearer may take knowledge of his discipline with some delight: and so apparel fair and good matter, that the studious of elegancy be not defrauded; redeem arts from their rough, and braky seats, where they lay hid, and overgrown with thorns, to a pure, open, and flowery light: where they may take the eye, and be taken by the hand.[4]

Chapter 2

Reading

Read not to contradict and confute; nor to believe and take for granted; nor to find talk and discourse; but to weigh and consider.
(Francis Bacon, 'Of Studies', *Essays*, 1625)

Texts and their contexts

Literature, as an academic subject, is not restricted to the study of characters, plots and images; it also enables us to investigate the intellectual climate, the social structures and the moral and emotional dilemmas of cultures past and present, familiar and strange. To understand Shakespeare or Emily Dickinson, we not only need to find out about the issues which concerned the Elizabethans and Jacobeans or the mid-nineteenth-century Americans, we also need to understand ourselves and our own society, and thus to enter into a dialogue with the text, transforming it and being transformed by it. Above all, we need to be aware that works of imaginative literature are written in the context of literature itself. Great writers have always been readers of this kind, boldly appropriating and reshaping the literature of the past in order to embody the spirit of their own age in daring and difficult contemporary fictions, a process already well established a couple of millennia ago when the Roman poet Virgil used Homer's story of the Trojan War as the starting point for his own epic, *The Aeneid*. His poem's most famous symbol, the golden bough which his hero Aeneas must find in order to descend into Avernus, the underworld kingdom of the dead, still retains its unique power over the imagination.

Quale solet sylvis brumali frigore viscum
Fronde virere nova, quod non sua seminat arbos,

Et croceo foetu teretes circumdare truncos.
Talis erat species auri frondentis opaca
Ilice, sic leni crepitabat bractea vento.[1]

                                    Like the mistletoe grown
From no parent seed, in the woods in the winter's coldness
Budding new leaf, circling the long round trunks with saffron –
Like that, in the black ilex, were the leaves of gold,
Tinkling so crisply in the breath of air.

The poet and critic Geoffrey Grigson, whose translation this is, said
of these lines, 'It is the physical humility of the mistletoe transformed; and it is life, naked, absolute and shining.'[2]

Thirteen centuries later, at the start of *The Divine Comedy*, Virgil's
countryman and fellow poet Dante encounters Virgil's ghost on the
threshold of Inferno, a place which is both Avernus and a medieval
Christian Hell. In a display of respectful modesty which is really a
shameless boast, the younger poet greets the older one:

Tu se' lo mio maestro e'l mio autore,
tu se' solo colui da cu' io tolsi
lo bello stilo che m'ha fatto onore.[3]

You are my master and my author.
It was from you alone I borrowed
The fine style that has brought me honour.

In fact Dante's boast is not nearly big enough. Far from simply
imitating Virgil's classical style in *The Divine Comedy*, he incorpor-
ated elements of Virgil's story material into an entirely new kind of
language for poetry, in which the topical and the scurrilous could
share a common space with the spiritual and the profound. He
called this language 'the vernacular', the rich and flexible dialect of
everyday speech which had never before been used by a Florentine
poet for epic poetry. The language of Dante's poem is still in use
today: we call it Italian.

At the beginning of the twentieth century, the Irish writer James
Joyce also turned, as Virgil had done nearly two thousand years
earlier, to the enduring stories of Homer to create his epic novel
Ulysses. Its extraordinary range of influences includes Dante, as well
as the classical and medieval poets and philosophers who left their

mark on *The Divine Comedy*. Joyce too was forging a new kind of language for literature, and his hero, Leopold Bloom, also goes down into the kingdom of the dead – in a spirit, this time, of mild scientific enquiry.

> Seat of the affections. Broken heart. A pump after all, pumping thousands of gallons of blood every day. One fine day it gets bunged up and there you are. Lots of them lying around here: lungs, hearts, livers. Old rusty pumps: damn the thing else. The resurrection and the life. Once you are dead you are dead. That last day idea. Knocking them all up out of their graves. Come forth, Lazarus! And he came fifth and lost the job. Get up! Last day! Then every fellow mousing around for his liver and his lights and the rest of his traps. Find damn all of himself that morning. Pennyweight of powder in a skull. Twelve grammes one pennyweight. Troy measure.[4]

Troy measure is the system of weights used for precious stones and metals, but Joyce does not mention it here only because it is precise enough to weigh that 'pennyweight of powder'. The day in June 1904 which Leopold Bloom spends wandering around Dublin is a comic modern version of the ten-year voyage of Homer's Odysseus, the hero whom both Virgil and Dante called Ulysses, whose cunning enabled the Greek chieftains to destroy the great city of Troy, which in turn sent the Trojan Aeneas on his own momentous journey.

But it is not only epic literature which survives the descent into Avernus. The minor seventeenth-century poet Edmund Waller sends a perhaps imaginary rose to a perhaps imaginary girl, and by some unaccountable alchemy his poem, doubtless intended as a far from original seduction piece, becomes a hauntingly enduring reflection on transience.

> Go lovely rose,
> Tell her that wastes her time and me
>   That now she knows
> When I resemble her to thee
> How sweet and fair she seems to be.
>
>   Tell her that's young
> And shuns to have her graces spied
>   That hadst thou sprung

In deserts where no men abide
Thou must have uncommended died.

   Small is the worth
Of beauty from the light retir'd,
   Bid her come forth,
Suffer herself to be desired
And not blush so to be admired.

   Then die that she
The common fate of all things rare
   May read in thee:
How small a part of time they share,
That are so wond'rous sweet and fair.

For all its apparent immediacy, Waller's poem too contains echoes of classical poetry. The tradition to which this kind of seduction poem belongs is often referred to by the Latin phrase 'carpe diem', which comes from one of Horace's Odes: *'carpe diem, quam minimum credula postero'* (take hold of the day, without counting too much on the morrow).[5] Though *'carpe'* here means seize and enjoy, the verb *carpere* is the one used for picking or gathering flowers and fruit. The Cumaean Sibyl uses it in this sense when she tells Aeneas to break off the golden bough from the dark holm oak. More appositely to Waller's poem, another great Roman poet, Ovid, uses it in his *Artis Amatoriae* (*The Arts of Love*) to express exactly the same message as 'Go lovely rose': *'carpite florem / Qui, nisi carptus erit, turpiter ipse cadet'* (gather the flower / Which, unless it is gathered, will fall into ugly decay).[6] Ovid's version is crueller than Waller's, threatening the woman who denies her lover with a frigid and lonely old age in which she will no longer wake to find her threshold strewn with roses; but there is a twist to Waller's treatment of the theme which a present-day reader could easily miss. The image of the rose had come to symbolize virginity, both in a religious sense when applied to the Virgin Mary and in a more directly physical one, so the final verse of Waller's *Song* hints at the real intention that lies behind the apparently innocent gift of a flower.

   However, there is another sense in which 'carpe diem' poems are only superficially about either sex or love; and indeed the Horace ode with which the phrase originates is concerned with neither. The underlying subject matter of such poems is time. Even in the

worldly and sensual context of the *Artis Amatoriae*, we find lines
which meditate on the briefness of youth and the inevitability of
age and death:

> *Dum licet, et vernos etiamnum educitis annos,*
>   *Ludite: eunt anni more fluentis aquae;*
> *Nec quae praeteriit, iterum revocabitur unda,*
>   *Nec quae praeteriit, hora redire potest.*

> As long as you may, and while you are still in your springtime,
>   Enjoy your sport; for the years flow by like water;
> And once it has gone, we are powerless to call back the wave,
>   Once it has gone, no hour can ever return.[7]

Robert Herrick's famous injunction, 'Gather ye Rose-buds while ye
may'[8] (note the opening verb), is not the only possible response to
such intimations of mortality. The nineteenth-century American poet
Emily Dickinson offers the opposite advice:

> Go not too near a House of Rose –
> The depredation of a Breeze
> Or inundation of a Dew
> Alarms its walls away –

> Nor try to tie the Butterfly,
> Nor climb the Bars of Ecstasy,
> In insecurity to lie
> Is Joy's insuring quality.

The early seventeenth century was one of the great ages of
English song-writing and, as its title suggests, Waller's poem was
really a song lyric. It was set by the composer Henry Lawes, who
also wrote the music for John Milton's masque *Comus*, in which a
Lady lost in a dark wood manages to preserve her virginity from the
wicked enchanter of the title, son of the beautiful witch Circe who
taught Odysseus how to summon and speak with the spirits of the
dead, the episode in Homer's *Odyssey* on which Virgil based Aeneas's
journey to the underworld. Waller belonged to the last generation of
poets who wrote love songs in quite this way. The great eighteenth-
century critic, poet and lexicographer, Samuel Johnson, commented
magisterially in his *Lives of the Poets* that Waller's 'amorous verses

have this to recommend them, that they are less hyperbolical than those of some other poets . . . There is however too much love, and too many trifles.'[9] By then, Waller's main claim to fame was the fact that his weightier poetry had helped to lead to the invention of that supremely eighteenth-century verse form, the Augustan couplet. Nowadays, 'Go lovely rose' is the single poem he is remembered by, and rightly so, for it perfectly epitomizes Ezra Pound's dictum that 'poetry atrophies when it gets too far from music'.[10]

It was a musical late eighteenth-century poet who unforgettably linked the image of the rose not with virginity but with fidelity. Robert Burns was born fifty years later than Samuel Johnson but outlived him only by twelve since, like the Romantic poet Byron, whom in some ways he resembled, he died in his thirties. Like Waller, he was a song writer as well as a poet, but his songs were written to help preserve the treasury of Scottish folk-tunes from being lost and their lyrics came from the folk idiom which, as the son of a tenant farmer, he had grown up with. In 'O my Luve's like a red, red rose', he uses that idiom to strip an idea down to its simplest expression. The novelist Walter Scott, who sincerely admired his poetry, felt that Burns had wasted his genius writing songs such as this:

> Notwithstanding the spirit of many of his lyrics, and the exquisite sweetness and simplicity of others, we cannot but regret that so much of his time and talents were frittered away in compiling and composing for musical collections . . . This constant waste of his power and fancy in small and insignificant compositions must necessarily have had no little effect in deterring him from undertaking any grave or important task.[11]

In fact, these songs have become a living legacy. While Waller is remembered for a single song lyric minus its tune, Burns fitted his words so convincingly to the airs he collected that many of them have remained an inseparable part of the folk tradition. I once heard the opening verse of this one being sung very tunefully in the geriatric ward of a Fife hospital, as a duet between an old man called Wullie Renfrew and a young student nurse. They were trying to settle an argument about whether it was or was not a hymn, and were quite unaware of how their mingled voices caused the third and fourth lines to enact their own metaphor.

O my Luve's like a red, red rose,
　　That's newly sprung in June;
O my Luve's like the melodie
　　That's sweetly play'd in tune.

As fair art thou, my bonie lass,
　　So deep in luve am I;
And I will love thee still, my Dear,
　　Till a' the seas gang dry.

Till a' the seas gang dry, my Dear,
　　And the rocks melt wi' the sun:
I will love thee still, my Dear,
　　While the sands o' life shall run.

And fare thee weel, my only Luve!
　　And fare thee weel a while!
And I will come again, my Luve,
　　Tho' it were ten thousand mile!

You can gauge the authenticity of this by comparing it with the opening stanzas of another of Burns's love songs, in which he mimics the mannered politeness of eighteenth-century English poetic diction to an extent that (perhaps intentionally) verges on the absurd:

Clarinda, mistress of my soul,
　　The measur'd time is run!
The wretch beneath the dreary pole,
　　So marks his latest sun.

To what dark cave of frozen night
　　Shall poor Sylvander hie;
Depriv'd of thee, his life and light,
　　The Sun of all his joy.

However, poetry can be authentic without necessarily being sincere and, far from loving a single lass 'till a' the seas gang dry', Burns was in real life a cheerfully shameless womanizer. Any reader naive enough to imagine that Wordsworth's description of Romantic poetry as 'the spontaneous overflow of powerful feelings' might also apply to romantic poetry with a lower-case *r* should read Burns's unabashed and affectionate celebration of the birth of his illegitimate daughter Elizabeth: *A Poet's Welcome to his love-begotten Daughter; the first instance that entitled him to the venerable appellation of Father −*. Later illegitimate children were to include two pairs of twins. As the jester Touchstone remarks in Shakespeare's *As You Like It*, 'the truest poetry is the most feigning; and lovers are given to poetry, and what they swear in poetry may be said as lovers they do feign'.[12]

Shakespeare, who could write almost anything except Petrarchan sonnets (the rhyme scheme of the Shakespearian sonnet makes it far less of a technical challenge), produced songs for every kind of dramatic situation. Some of these, such as 'Who is Sylvia?' and 'Hark, hark, the lark', are really art songs, laid on to provide a decorative interlude, but the most interesting and experimental ones are what in film studies is called 'diegetic music': the kind of music which appears to arise naturally out of the action on the stage or screen. This fictitious naturalness sometimes involves a degree of realism surprising in Elizabethan and Jacobean drama. Instead of elaborating on a moment of strong emotion, as an operatic aria might do, or highlighting some key feature of the plot, these songs appear to be autonomously chosen, reflecting not the action of the drama but the psychology of the singer. For example, in *Twelfth Night*, Feste the clown is asked to sing to his employer's disreputable uncle Toby and his dim-witted friend and dupe Sir Andrew Aguecheek who are slumming it below stairs in the small hours.[13] All three in their different ways − wry, belligerent, querulous − are disappointed in life. All three are drunk. The song, 'O mistress mine', mirrors neither the situation of the characters nor that of the main plot lovers, but its very inappropriateness is a stroke of genius. The familiar theme of the song − that 'in delay there lies no plenty' since 'youth's a stuff will not endure' − is also the preoccupation from which the middle-aged and disillusioned take refuge in drink, only to find that very thought, magnified by maudlin emotion, lying at the bottom of the emptied glass. The destroying action of time on youth and beauty is a major theme of Shakespeare's sonnets: here the banality of the hearers is brought home by the sweetness of the song.

In Shakespeare's last plays, this realism gives way to something stranger. Ferdinand, in *The Tempest*, hears an unearthly music in which his drowned father undergoes a transformation, a 'sea change' which mimics the decay it preserves him from: 'those are pearls that were his eyes'. By enacting an event which the audience knows not to have taken place (since Alonso has drowned only in Ferdinand's imagination), the song functions in an almost supernatural way, creating a space in which things feared take on a dreamlike actuality. This time the song does arise out of the plot – the magician Prospero's plot as well as Shakespeare's – but it mirrors it backwards. A similar kind of plot reversal happens in the song from *Cymbeline* which is often referred to as Fidele's dirge. A dirge is a funeral song, but the page boy Fidele who is the subject, not the singer, of this one is not really called Fidele, is not really a boy and is not really dead. Nor, in the event, does anyone actually sing his dirge. *Cymbeline* is perhaps the most perplexing of Shakespeare's plays, and has been categorized as a history, a comedy and even a tragedy with a happy ending, though these days it is usually grouped with the other three late plays, *Pericles*, *The Winter's Tale* and *The Tempest*, as a romance. Johnson, who edited Shakespeare's plays during the Age of Reason, sums up in one tremendous sentence the irrationality of its plot:

> To remark the folly of the fiction, the absurdity of the conduct, the confusion of the names and manners of different times, and the impossibility of the events in any system of life, were to waste criticism upon unresisting imbecility, upon faults too evident for detection, and too gross for aggravation.[14]

Shakespeare never invented story material if he could borrow it, and in *Cymbeline* he borrowed from such disparate boxes that a Renaissance-style Italian villain, who emerges like a sinister jack-in-the-box from a trunk in the heroine's bedroom, intent on raping not her but her reputation, is forced to share the playing space with an invading Roman army and a pair of Ancient British princes, stolen in infancy and brought up in a Welsh cave by the kidnapper they believe to be their father. It is they who lay out Fidele's body, intending to 'sing him to the ground' – unaware that this is in fact their sister Imogen (or possibly Innogen – Shakespeare's illegible handwriting may have misled the printer) who has disguised herself as a boy because the husband she passionately loves has been deceived by the villain in the trunk into planning her murder, and who is currently in a deathlike trance on account of a mishap with a wicked stepmother and a box of poison. All this might seem to bear out Johnson's point, and in a sense it does, but reason is not an infallible guide to the workings of the imagination and here too Shakespeare has created a dreamlike actuality, one in which a universal grief can be both summoned up and allayed. Since one of the brothers is prevented from singing by his tears, the words of the song are spoken antiphonally over what, as far as the audience is aware at this point, may well be Imogen's dead body. This is a device which may have been forced on Shakespeare by the breaking voice of one or both of the boy actors playing the stolen princes, but the fact that this is a song without music adds to the haunting inevitability of the words.

> Fear no more the heat o' th' sun,
>   Nor the furious winter's rages,
> Thou thy worldly task has done,
>   Home art gone and ta'en thy wages.
> Golden lads and girls all must,
> As chimney-sweepers, come to dust.
>
> Fear no more the frown o' th' great,
>   Thou art past the tyrant's stroke.
> Care no more to clothe and eat,
>   To thee the reed is as the oak:
> The sceptre, learning, physic, must
> All follow this and come to dust.
>
> Fear no more the lightning-flash
>   Nor th' all-dreaded thunder-stone.
> Fear not slander, censure rash.
>   Thou hast finished joy and moan.
> All lovers young, all lovers must
> Consign to thee and come to dust.
>
> No exorciser harm thee!
> Nor no witchcraft charm thee!
> Ghost unlaid forbear thee!
> Nothing ill come near thee!
> Quiet consummation have,
> And renowned be thy grave![15]

We usually think of exorcism as the power to lay ghosts, but here an exorcizer is someone who, like Homer's Circe, has the power to raise them, so the final six lines of the song are a spell to make certain that

Fidele will rest quietly in his grave. In the mirror logic governing Shakespeare's late plays, this spell ensures that Imogen will wake.

Virginia Woolf's novels are full of Shakespearian echoes, partly because, as a woman writer, she felt the need to measure herself against him; she memorably describes, in *A Room of One's Own*, how Shakespeare's imaginary sister Judith might have fared in Elizabethan London if she had tried to shape her life according to her genius rather than her gender. In *Mrs Dalloway*, she uses Fidele's dirge to link a brittle society hostess with a shell-shocked and eventually suicidal young man she never meets, turning Shakespeare's song in the process into a charm or lullaby against fear.

> Outside the trees dragged their leaves like nets through the depths of the air; the sound of water was in the room, and through the waves came the voices of birds singing. Every power poured its treasures on his head, and his hand lay there on the back of the sofa, as he had seen his hand lie when he was bathing, floating, on the top of the waves, while far away on shore he heard dogs barking and barking far away. Fear no more, says the heart in the body; fear no more.[16]

Joyce called such vivid fleeting impressions 'epiphanies'; Woolf called them 'moments of being' and made them the centre of her art. Often, as here, they are intertextual moments in which a thought or a feeling is brought into sharp focus through the lens of a fragment of verse. In what is arguably her greatest novel, *To the Lighthouse*, she uses Shakespeare's Sonnet 98 to explore the emotional dynamics of a marriage. Earlier in the summer day which occupies the opening section of the novel, Mr Ramsay has been planning a lecture in which 'he would argue . . . that the arts are merely a decoration imposed on the top of human life; they do not express it. Nor is Shakespeare necessary to it.'[17] As he sits after dinner and watches his wife reading, longing for her attention but reluctant to interrupt her, he is unaware that the poem she finally settles on is one which contains his own feelings about the absence of the beloved; but the sonnet, in its technical perfection, also expresses Mrs Ramsay's solitary inner self, which, like Andrew Marvell's in *The Garden*, 'from pleasures less, / Withdraws into its happiness'.[18]

> She was climbing up those branches, this way and that, laying hands on one flower and then another.

> Nor praise the deep vermilion in the rose,

she read, and so reading she was ascending, she felt, on to the top, on to the summit. How satisfying! How restful! All the odds and ends of the day stuck to this magnet; her mind felt swept, felt clean. And then there it was, suddenly entire shaped in her hands, beautiful and reasonable, clear and complete, the essence sucked out of life and held rounded here – the sonnet.[19]

Laying down her book, she murmurs the closing line: 'As with your shadow I with these did play.'

The scene casts its own forward shadow, since this is the last time the reader will see Mrs Ramsay alive; and the key words 'shadow' and 'vermilion' connect Sonnet 98 with Lily Briscoe's painting, the completion of which will also complete the novel. In the first version of the painting, Mrs Ramsay is reduced to a triangular purple shadow which is none the less essential to the balance of the entire composition. When, ten years later, Lily tries to reconstruct her original vision, it is the accident of some unknown person sitting at the same window and casting the same 'odd-shaped triangular shadow over the step'[20] which conjures up Mrs Ramsay herself to bring closure to Lily's anguish over her death. As for vermilion, it is a synthetic form of cinnabar, one of the pigments of the ancient world, and produces a brilliant red paint which in the early Middle Ages, when it was used in illuminated manuscripts, was as expensive as gold leaf. By the Renaissance it had become cheap enough to be used lavishly, and seventy years after Shakespeare's death the discovery of a new production method made it cheaper still but changed the blueish-red pigment produced by the ancient process into an orange-red, which is why the 'deep vermilion' of Shakespeare's rose is crimson while Gerard Manley Hopkins's 'blue-bleak embers' which 'fall, gall themselves, and gash gold-vermilion'[21] are flame-coloured.[22] Though the words come out of quite different linguistic boxes, it is a shared intensity of colour which links the image of the rose in Shakespeare's sonnet with the one in Burns's song. Lily's painting depends on the use of saturated colour, which to her is not superficial or decorative but a way of expressing the deep structures she perceives in the visible world:

> She could have done it differently of course; the colour could have been thinned and faded; the shapes etherealized . . . But she

did not see it like that. She saw the colour burning on a frame-
work of steel; the light of a butterfly's wing lying upon the
arches of a cathedral.[23]

In the central section of the novel, the narrative concerns itself
with the destructive effects of time on the inanimate objects which
fill the Ramsays' now deserted holiday house, with the few references
to the characters themselves appearing in square brackets. In the first
of these, 'Mr Carmichael, who was reading Virgil, blew out his
candle' because 'It was past midnight',[24] while in the second:

[Mr Ramsay stumbling along a passage stretched his arms out
one dark morning, but, Mrs Ramsay having died rather suddenly the night before, he stretched his arms out. They remained empty.][25]

This too is an intertextual moment of being, and it tells us the very
lines of Book VI of Virgil's *Aeneid* on which Mr Carmichael closed
his book. It is the passage where Aeneas, meeting his father's spirit in
the Elysian Fields, tries vainly three times to embrace him, but three
times the ghost escapes from his hands, '*Par levibus ventis, volucrique
simillima somno*' (Just like insubstantial winds or a fleeting dream).[26]
You will not be surprised by now to discover that Virgil did not invent these lines, he stole them from the episode in Homer's *Odyssey*
in which the hero tries to clasp his dead mother, who three times
slips from his arms like a shadow or a dream.[27] In order to understand Mr Ramsay's analogous gesture, we need to remember that
Virginia Woolf's novel was an autobiographical one, written partly
as a long-delayed response to her painful memories of her mother's
death and her father's paralysing grief. To lay these ghosts to rest it
was necessary first to summon them up. Her sister Vanessa Bell, on
reading the novel for the first time, found 'the rising of the dead
almost painful',[28] while Woolf herself records in her diary, 'I used to
think of him & mother daily, but writing *The Lighthouse* laid them in
my mind.'[29] The chilling glimpse of Mr Ramsay 'stumbling along a
passage' is above all something seen and indelibly remembered, but
those few lines of classical poetry help her to make emotional sense
of it, both for herself and the reader. Learning to develop a keen ear
for such echoes enables us to understand that 'classical references' are
not merely ornamental or elitist features of a text but can be literally
a matter of life and death.

Studying literature at university does not necessarily mean starting out with a great store of knowledge, but it does mean being alert and curious and prepared to be attentive to a wide range of voices from different times and cultures; and it also means sharing with the writers of the past and present the rigours and the pleasures of learning to use words well. John Milton thought that it was the vocation of the poet 'To scorn delights, and live laborious days',[30] but the twentieth-century writer T. H. White describes in his small masterpiece *The Goshawk*, a strangely compelling book about his obsessive attempt to train a wild and beautiful bird of prey, how he once found himself involuntarily recollecting Milton's line, except that 'it presented itself the other way about, saying: *To live laborious days for their delight*'.[31]

Critical reading

All writing about literature has to begin with reading, and the way you read a text may either open it up for you or limit the ways in which you are able to think about it, correspondingly expanding or restricting the possible scope of your essay long before you begin to write it or even decide on its topic. Indeed, preconceived ideas about what literature consists of may circumscribe your experience of the text before you even open the book. For instance, if you think of novels as being primarily about characters and their relationships, and of reading poetry as largely a matter of responding to imagery, then those will be the aspects which your reading will foreground. You will notice Jane Austen's attitude to her heroines' marriage prospects but not her interest in their fictionality, and register the beauty of Shakespeare's sonnets but not, for instance, his fascination with legal metaphors. We all read books, as indeed we 'read' everything we encounter, through the invisible lenses which history and society have given us. We cannot remove those lenses, since without their aid we would not be able to make sense of the world at all. The real value of creative literature is that, by observing the many and diverse ways in which novelists, poets and dramatists engage with that world, we can begin to see more creatively ourselves. An adventurous approach to the possibilities offered by critical reading can transform your vision of more than just the printed page, and this in turn will affect the ways in which you as a writer engage with literary texts and their contexts.

One common reason for reading in a conservative way is an understandable suspicion about the whole enterprise of literary criticism. People who became students of literature in the first place because of their love of books often start to worry that reading a text critically will mean replacing that enjoyment with an intellectually challenging but essentially meaningless hunt for barren themes and symbols. This idea can make you feel about the whole critical enterprise as Wordsworth, in a negative moment, felt about people who sit indoors studying natural history instead of striding romantically out into the landscape to engage with what he took to be Nature herself:

> Our meddling intellect
> Misshapes the beauteous forms of things –
> We murder to dissect.[32]

If you imagine that reading a text critically means tearing it apart, murdering it to dissect it, then it is natural to try to avoid this by deciding to do the reading purely for its own sake and postpone the critical process until later. However, this means that when you come to plan your essay you will be doing all your critical thinking about a text experienced retrospectively via the memory of a reading during which you may well have been mainly concerned with suspending your disbelief in the reality of the characters or losing yourself in the incantation of the words. And since there is no such thing as a value-free reading of any text, attempting to defer your critical judgement is only too likely simply to make you revert to a mind-set you prepared earlier, slipping easily and unknowingly back into ways of thinking which enabled your younger self to compare and contrast two poems by Philip Larkin or write a character study of Lady Macbeth.

   Literary texts are meaningful on many different levels, not all of which can be discovered in any one reading by any one reader. They are also meaningful in different ways at different historical periods. Milton saw Shakespeare as 'fancy's child' warbling 'his native wood-notes wild'.[33] John Dryden called him 'the very *Janus* of Poets; he wears, almost everywhere two faces: and you have scarce begun to admire the one e're you despise the other'.[34] Samuel Johnson thought of him as 'the poet who holds up to his readers a faithful mirrour of manners and of life', and commented approvingly, 'In the writings of other poets a character is too often an individual; in those of Shakespeare it is commonly a species.'[35] (No character studies of Lady Macbeth for him.) When, in 1673, the actor William Cademan had the stage version of *Macbeth: A Tragedy Acted At the Dukes-Theatre* printed 'at the Popes-Head in the New Exchange, in the Strand', he didn't even bother to ensure that the author's name was included on the title page, and the Dukes Theatre revival of Shakespeare's by now old-fashioned tragedy had been spiced up with lively song and dance routines for the witches.

> Sometimes about a hollow Tree
> A Round, a Round, a Round Dance we:
> Thither a chirping Critick comes,
> And beetles singing drowsie hums.[36]

The typo which transformed the 'chirping Crickit' into a Critick effectively sees off any objections from later purists.

There is no right and fixed and timeless way of reading Shakespeare, and none of the great writers of the past, however admiring of him in terms of the literary values of their own age, can tell us how to read him in the twenty-first century. There is no way either of recapturing the experience of the groundlings who stood through the first performances of the plays – not even by going to the reconstructed Globe Theatre with its earnest auditors clutching their Penguin Shakespeares. Nor would the original Elizabethan or Jacobean audience recognize our Shakespeare, that gold standard of the national curriculum, in the popular dramatist who entertained them with ingenious comedies and blood-boltered tragedies ripped off from printed sources and put together against the clock. And what goes for reading Shakespeare goes for reading the work of any other writer. The only way that we can make a text new is by reading it inventively, not imposing a preconceived pattern on it but discovering within it patterns relevant to the concerns of our own culture.

At the same time, though, we have to take care that we do not falsify the text itself by misreading it. This is a particular danger when reading poetry. It is possible for highly intelligent students (or, indeed, well-known and much-published professors) to read a poem so ingeniously that they misunderstand, at the simplest level, what it is actually about: failing to realize, for example, that John Clare's *Little Trotty Wagtail* describes a bird, the pied wagtail, rather than a dog, or that Wallace Stevens' poem *The Auroras of Autumn* takes its title from the Aurora Borealis – the Northern Lights which drape the night sky with luminous streamers of colour – rather than the Roman goddess of dawn.[37] If we think of poems as being like riddles, which indeed they often resemble, then in order to solve them we need to be attentive to all the clues they contain, which includes thinking carefully about mundane things such as word order and even punctuation, not least because in the magical economy of the poem these things are not mundane at all. The linguist Noam Chomsky famously invented a couple of meaningless sentences to illustrate his belief that knowledge of grammatical structures is hard-wired into the human brain:

> Sentences (1) and (2) are equally nonsensical but any speaker of English will recognize that only the former is grammatical.
> (1) Colorless green ideas sleep furiously.
> (2) Furiously sleep ideas green colorless.[38]

This is indeed the case if we think of Chomsky's two sentences as prose. However, if we impose the grammar and logic of poetry on to sentence number two, we will find that, by giving it a suitable context (and taking advantage of the fact that, felicitously, it scans) we can make it become far from meaningless:

> Furiously sleep ideas, green, colourless.
> Dreaming, the mind seethes with the shoals they make,
> Till they lie beached in daylight's shallow water –
> Green while they slept, colourless when we wake.

In the liberties that they take with language, poems often operate at the frontiers where sense and nonsense meet, and to decode them we have to become linguists ourselves – linguists of riddles – since undecoded they cannot be interpreted.

Reading critically means developing an instinct that there is something there to be looked for. It may be a something that you can begin to unmask by asking a simple question: who was Hecate, and why does Shakespeare associate her with a trio of Scottish witches? Why does Marvell, in the closing lines of *Upon Appleton House*, describe salmon fishers carrying their coracles on their heads as 'like Antipodes in shoes'?[39] What did the little musical phrase which runs through Proust's *A la recherche du temps perdu* actually sound like? It may be a something which suddenly strikes you and illuminates your view of the text, and for which you then have to find convincing evidence. It may be a something which you can only piece together by collating the results of patient close reading. Whatever your questions and discoveries, learning to look beyond the obvious can only enrich your enjoyment of literature as well as improving your essays about it, since novels and poems and plays become more meaningful and exciting the more intelligently we read them.

Reading the critics

It is often taken for granted that any questioning of a work of literature about which a student is going to write should take place at one remove, by reading literary criticism. This can lead to an overly dependent essay-writing strategy in which the student, having dutifully read the text, then also reads every relevant critical book to be found on the library shelves and tries to assimilate as many of the opinions they contain as possible – not an easy task, since their authors will certainly not all be in agreement with each other. The resulting essay is likely to be largely held together by quotations from the secondary reading, with few quotations from the text other than those which the secondary reading has itself provided, and inevitably the whole thing will feel second-hand and passive. As an apprentice critic, you can certainly learn a lot from academic books and articles, not least by using your budding critical skills to figure out what makes their arguments exciting and persuasive, or conversely dull and unconvincing, but you should neither expect nor allow them to do your thinking for you. Being a critic, even an apprentice one, demands a readiness to engage personally with the text. You can make much better use of published criticism if you have already formed some opinions of your own. Indeed, the critics you disagree with can often be the most helpful, since they enable you to test out the strength of your own ideas against a forcefully argued opposing point of view.

The study of literature as a discipline has changed considerably over the last few decades, with much greater emphasis on what literary texts have to tell us about their historical, social and political contexts, as well as a preoccupation with the interface between literary studies and other disciplines such as linguistics, philosophy or psychology, so it is sensible to begin your reading of literary criticism with books and articles published fairly recently. However, reading criticism from a range of periods can help to give you an idea of the history of the reception of a text, enabling you to look at its current place in the canon with a little more perspective. Either way, it is wise to check the original publication date of any critical book or article you read since all critics, however original or dispassionate, reflect the spirit of the age in which they write. The contents of a book about Fanny Burney or Maria Edgeworth dating from before the rise of women's studies, which led to their reappraisal as signific-ant writers, may tell you more about social attitudes in the 1950s or 1960s than it does about pre-Victorian women novelists, but recent books on the same writers, which may seem to share your own preconceptions, are not necessarily completely objective either. It is up to you to judge the agenda and the unspoken subtext of any work of criticism you read.

Finally, one of the most valuable parts of any book of criticism is its bibliography, which provides you not just with an inventory of the publications which the author made use of in researching his or her subject but also with a helpful resource for pursuing your own ideas. You are likely to notice that the bibliography of any stimulat-ing and imaginative work of criticism does not confine itself to the books and articles of other critics in the same field but includes a wide range of other printed material, some of it quite eclectic and unexpected. One problem with less recent criticism is that its writers often failed to give adequate bibliographical details for the passages they quoted or referred to, forcing their readers to play a game of hunt the thimble through the complete works of the cited author (only too often a prolific one, such as Ruskin or Henry James) if they wanted to trace some teasingly useful-sounding passage to its source. Contemporary anxieties about intellectual property rights, which have paradoxically accompanied the internet revolution, have at least led to much more meticulous referencing and indexing, while the growing number of machine-searchable on-line texts has simplified the hunt for the unattributed quotation.

Background reading

Even really intelligent and hard-working students often take the term 'background reading' literally, ranking the possible kinds of preparatory reading by their proximity to the texts they intend to write about. According to this way of thinking, the text itself occu-pies the foreground, and ranged behind it, in decreasing order of importance, are critical essays about the text, other poems, novels or plays by the author of the text, biographies of and letters and journals by that author, and finally, lurking neglected in the shadows, some-thing called 'historical background reading'. Not surprisingly, this kind of reading seldom gets done. Students often feel slightly guilty about this, and some even make a propitiatory gesture towards actually doing it by going to the library and finding a book called something like *Tudor and Jacobean England*, or *Nineteenth Century France* or *The First World War*, but the specific demands of preparing for and writing their essays crowd out the time it would take to read them. In any case, especially if you are wedded to the idea that novels and plays are about characters and poems are about imagery, it can be quite hard to see what a bit of general knowledge about Jacobean England or nineteenth-century France could add to your analysis of marital tensions in *Macbeth* or *Madame Bovary*, or even how an understanding of the causes of the First World War could deepen your appreciation of Wilfred Owen. Surely all you need to know about the pity and horror of war is contained in the poems themselves.

It would be easy to counter this by saying that any educated person ought to know a bit of European history but, though true, this wouldn't really be helpful. If you come to that, all educated people ought to know a bit about Darwin's theory of evolution and Einstein's theory of relativity, not to mention the periodic table and the genome project, chaos theory and string theory and what happens inside a black hole, but it is a sad fact of life that many of them don't and never will. In an ideal university in an ideal world, humanities professors and their students would be as knowledgeable and keen about maths and science and technology as many science professors, and at least some of their students, already are about music and the arts. If you have aspirations (and perhaps you should) towards becoming a Renaissance man or woman, you can make a sensible start by reading *New Scientist* every week, but that isn't going to get your essay down on paper. However, radically revising your ideas about the nature and scope of background reading really could help you to do so.

The real purpose of background reading (which may or may not be historical) is not to let you bulk out the introduction to your essay with a few facts about the period in which your author lived but, on the contrary, to enable you to foreground those aspects of a text which you would otherwise be unable to get sufficiently close to. Sometimes, when you have stumbled on a textual puzzle which has been neglected by all the critics to whose work you have access, there is no other effective way of doing this. At other times, it may be precisely a hint from a critic which sets you on the right trail. In order to track down the complex answers to the simple questions raised by your critical reading, you may need to find out about James I's interest in witchcraft, or seventeenth-century notions of geography and astronomy, or the music of Ravel and Debussy (in which case reading will need to be supplemented by listening), and all these things will take you to areas of the library other than the literature shelves. The section on 'Libraries and librarians' in the next chapter will give you some ideas about how to find what you are looking for. The keyword search facility in the on-line catalogue of your university library should enable you to create your own booklist, which you can then narrow down to the real possibilities by intelligent skimming of the books themselves. Incidentally, however large the pile of relevant books you end up with, it doesn't necessarily mean that you have a lot of reading to do. Sometimes you will only have to consult the index and read a few pages to access the information you need; sometimes you will need to read a chapter or more; often it will be necessary to collate the results of different kinds of reading.

Take, for example, Joseph Conrad's brilliant and disturbing story *Heart of Darkness*, in which an out-of-work British seaman called Marlow signs up, in a sinister and unnamed European city, for an ill-defined assignment and finds himself steering a ramshackle boat up an equally sinister and unnamed river in the heart of equatorial Africa, in search of a mysterious ivory trader called Kurtz. While it is quite hard to read Conrad's novella in terms of the relationships between the characters – not least because no such relationships exist – it is only too easy to read it as a generalized parable against colonialism, though one in which Conrad at least partly undermines his own case through his unwillingness to relinquish a belief in the altruism of the British Empire. Any critic writing about *Heart of Darkness* will tell you that the city in the tale is Brussels and the river is the Congo, but in order really to understand why Conrad has Kurtz die with the words 'The horror! The horror!' on his lips, you need to put together two different kinds of background reading. A biography of Conrad will tell you how a young Polish revolutionary called Józef Korzeniowski, who became a French-speaking seaman, later came to write a fictionalized account, in the English he was always to speak with a strong southern French accent, of his own glimpse of atrocities in the Belgian Congo. It will also give you a sense of the ironic distance between Conrad and Marlow, his English protagonist and narrator. However, you need a historical account of those atrocities, in all their unspeakable brutality, to enable you to understand that the horror in Conrad's tale is not just some allegorized reflection on the blackness of the human heart.

Incidentally, if it occurs to you to wonder, as you read, why Europe, at the end of the nineteenth century, had such a cruel and insatiable hunger for African ivory, finding a list of its mundane and often trivial commercial uses will enable you to decode one of the key images in the story: the great black piano which dominates the room in Brussels where Marlow meets the beautiful, deluded young woman who was Kurtz's intended bride. The ivory has already been linked with art: Kurtz, on his stretcher, resembles 'an animated image of death carved out of old ivory'.[40] Now, in the oppressive room in Brussels where the Intended's 'pale head, floating towards' Marlow 'in the dusk'[41] recalls the bleached whiteness of a skull, the coffin-lid of the sarcophagus piano is closed to conceal the death's head grin of its ivory keys.

Chapter 3

Research

Looking things up

Research is rather an alarming word. It suggests dedicated workers in white coats patiently decoding the human genome, and embattled professors of literature honing their forensic skills in order to identify or debunk the putative lost works of Shakespeare. It may never have occurred to you that research is something that you, as a student essay-writer, ought to be doing. But research does not always mean taking elaborate steps to find out new things. It often means taking quite simple steps to find out things which are known to a lot of people already. The kind of research which I want to talk about here could be described as the art of looking things up.

Students who are assiduous about reading the text, critical commentaries on the text, and other texts by the same author, often feel comfortably sure that there is nothing more they need do in order to understand the text and its contexts. This is far from being the case. One of the most exciting things about the study of literature is that there is no kind of knowledge that is not relevant to it. Poets and novelists and playwrights expect from us a knowledge, both specific and diverse, of history, geography, natural history, philosophy, theology, the history of science, even of mathematics. They expect us to have read our Bible and our Homer and our Plato; to know what a windhover is, and what a skylark, a nightingale and a nightjar sound like; to be informed about coracles and mandrakes and ambergris and the divine right of kings and the mosaics at Ravenna; to have some acquaintance with lamias and changelings, with alchemists and astronomers and Fellows of the Royal Society. They expect us to know about these things, not because they are perverse or elitist, but because literature is about what it means to be human, and to be human is to be acted upon by the society, the world, the universe, the time and the eternity in which we live, and in which we imagine that we live.

Finding out about these things, at its simplest level, means knowing where to look them up, which may well involve consulting more than one source of information. The student who thought that T. S. Eliot 'links the thrush in the opening section of "Burnt Norton" with both children and deception because of the bird's well-known habit of laying its eggs in other birds' nests' could have put herself right simply by consulting a book on British birds. However, the large number of students who wrongly believe that Gerard Manley Hopkins' sonnet *The Windhover* is about a falcon would need the curiosity to look up its title in the *Oxford English Dictionary* as a prelude to reaching for that bird book, while the student who thought that W. B. Yeats's poem *Leda and the Swan* describes 'an anonymous girl being overwhelmed by a Jungian symbol of sexual passion' would have had to begin by feeding the two proper names Yeats mentions, Leda and Agamemnon, into an on-line search engine in order to discover that it was two stories from Greek mythology and the link between them (Leda's daughter Helen, whose abduction caused the Trojan war) which he needed information about. The following advice about reference books and other information sources will give you at least a start in the business of looking things up; though it is important to remember too that sometimes the information you need is out there in the real world. The student who thought that, in Ovid's telling of the story of Philomela, 'she is turned into a bird and can only give voice to her pain through the ugly song of the nightingale' could best have discovered his mistake by standing in a wood at night, as Keats describes doing in his *Ode to a Nightingale*, and listening to the bird itself – or failing that (since the British nightingale population is in decline and is now mainly confined to the south-east of England) by listening to a recording of it.

Dictionaries

Since literature is made out of words, such a list must begin with dictionaries, among which *The Oxford English Dictionary*, in twenty enormous volumes or on CD-ROM, is the most authoritative. This gives you the etymology of each word, followed by detailed definitions, illustrated by quotations, of all its possible meanings, past and present. This information about obsolete meanings makes it an essential tool for the student of literature, who has to know, for instance, that George Herbert's rose, with 'hue angry and brave',[1] was a red and resplendent one, and that Andrew Marvell's *Nymph Complaining for the Death of her Fawn* was lamenting, not grumbling.

You can buy the *OED* shrunk down to two volumes and supplied with a magnifying glass, but for most people it remains a work to be consulted in libraries or on-line. However, you will certainly need to buy a smaller dictionary for those routine checks on meaning and spelling without which reading and writing cannot be really precise. I would recommend *The Concise Oxford Dictionary*. There is a CD-ROM version of this (which sometimes comes free with computer magazines) but, unless you are in the habit of reading with a laptop on your knee, the paper version is more user-friendly. If you can afford it, the more capacious *Chambers Dictionary* is also highly recommended. The pocket dictionary you had at school is not sufficient, and do not let economy tempt you into buying a paperback dictionary which, however excellent its contents, will fall apart if consulted too often.

Even the *OED* by no means contains all the words in the English language, and on occasion you may need to consult dialect dictionaries, dictionaries of slang, of the technical terms used in different disciplines, of place-names, surnames and first names, even of clichés. These all exist and are to be found in university libraries, along with bilingual and monolingual dictionaries in a rich assortment of foreign languages. (For advice on choosing and using foreign language dictionaries, see the section on 'Real-life language learning' in Chapter 9.)

Roget's Thesaurus, which lists the possible synonyms of a word, is an invaluable tool for the translator but only occasionally useful for the essay-writer. Despite the name, thesauruses come in many different versions and sizes, though (except for the *Oxford Thesaurus*, which is alphabetical) they are mostly still based on the ordering system by subject invented in the mid nineteenth century by the Anglo-French polymath Peter Mark Roget. As with dictionaries, you should avoid pocket versions. You should also be aware that a thesaurus is *not* a dictionary, and can seriously mislead you if you mistake it for one. It can be worth consulting if you know what you want to say but are stuck for the right word, but overmuch reliance on it is like writing poetry with the help of a rhyming dictionary. It can also seduce you into 'lacy' language, of which more later.

Biblical references

Another book which you would be well advised to buy is the Bible. It may not have occurred to you to think of this as a reference book, but for the student of literature it is an essential one, enabling you to examine the source material for Milton's *Samson Agonistes* (Judges, chs 13–16) and for Father Mapple's sermon in Herman Melville's *Moby-Dick* (Jonah, chs 1–2), to find out where Henry James got his title for *The Wings of the Dove* (Psalm 55, verses 4–13) and D. H. Lawrence his for *The Rainbow* (Genesis, ch 9, verses 12–15). There are many English translations of the Bible, but the one which you need for this purpose is the Authorized King James Version, which you can recognize, if you are unfamiliar with its language, by the dedicatory address to King James I at the beginning. (Don't be misled into buying the New King James Version instead.) This translation, which is a magnificent work of art in its own right, has coloured English language and literature for nearly four hundred years. For literary purposes you can't make do with the New English Bible or Good News Bible, since these translations will not give you the actual words which generations of writers in English were echoing.

King James Bibles come in many shapes and sizes; indeed, if you have ever been a bridesmaid you may already own an unreadably tiny copy in dainty white and silver binding. For research purposes, though, you need one with large clear print, bound in stiff covers rather than limp leatherette, and free from coloured pictures of shepherds watching their flocks by night. You should also avoid editions with 'the Words of Christ in red letter', a piece of printerly piety which can make the Gospels quite difficult to read. I would recommend The Holy Bible: King James Version, Standard Text Edition (Cambridge University Press).

You don't, of course, have to limit your biblical researches to a single translation, however splendid; and in fact the King James Version itself is not a single translation but a composite one, largely based on the brilliant, pioneering work of William Tyndale (burned at the stake in 1536 for what was then seen as a politically and theologically subversive enterprise) but supplemented with material from other translations, including the latinate Catholic Douai Bible (whose translators added 'words like victim, allegory, acquisition and adulterate'[2] to the English language) and the scholarly Protestant Geneva Bible (read by Shakespeare in his youth). All of these translations would be worth investigating, while interesting modern versions include William Laughton Lorimer's vivid and masterly New Testament in Scots[3] and the even more vivid Lion Graphic Bible[4] by Jeff Anderson and Mike Maddox, a comic book version which reliably promises 'more fights, muscles and villains than Batman and Superman together'.[5] Beware, however, of anything claiming to be a Student Bible, which will almost certainly be trying to impose its own moral agenda on both the reader and the text.

King James I's committees of Biblical scholars also turned their attention to the Apocrypha, the collection of 'Old Testament books that the early Christian churches had accepted as sacred but the rabbis of the period of the destruction of Jerusalem had rejected'.[6] Nowadays, the Apocrypha is excluded from Protestant Bibles (though you can buy it as a separate volume) but usefully included in Catholic ones. You will need to turn to the Apocrypha if you want to read the story of Judith and Holofernes or Susanna and the Elders or find out what Shadrach, Meshach and Abednego sang in 'the midst of the burning fiery furnace'.[7]

A Biblical concordance, such as Strong's *Concordance of the Bible*, will enable you to trace biblical references to their source, while *The Literary Guide to the Bible*, edited by Robert Alter and Frank Kermode,[8] gives you a scholarly and readable introduction, from a literary rather than a theological viewpoint, to every book in the Bible.

Classical references

For classical references, you need *The Oxford Classical Dictionary*. You could also look at Lemprière's *Classical Dictionary*, which was used by Keats. Ovid's great poem *Metamorphoses* can be used as a reference book on Greek myths, though unfortunately there is no really satisfactory modern English translation. Of those currently in print, A. D. Melville's blank verse version[9] probably has the edge on Mary Innes's prose one,[10] but neither is exactly inspired; however, they do both include a useful index of proper names. The Loeb Classical Library edition gives you a parallel text, though the translation is elderly and quaint.[11] (Loeb editions are currently being updated, though, so that may change.) It is also worth looking at Arthur Golding's lively and still readable sixteenth-century verse translation, which was used by Shakespeare (whose Latin, if Ben Jonson is to be believed, was not up to much, though better than his Greek). No such problem with Homer, another vital source of classical story material; Robert Fagles' powerful translations of *The Iliad* and *The Odyssey*[12] are the ones to read.

Oral literature

If the story material you are looking for belongs to the vast corpus of British oral literature, a good place to start is the *Oxford Dictionary of English Folklore*. In addition, Katharine Briggs is an authority on British folk-tales and fairy lore, while Iona and Peter Opie, the great anthropologists of the playground, are a mine of information on children's games, rhymes and riddles, and have also edited useful collections of *Classic Fairy Tales* and *Nursery Rhymes*. Bertrand H. Bronson's *The Traditional Tunes of the Child Ballads*[13] gives you the music as well as the words of *The English and Scottish Popular Ballads*, collected at the end of the nineteenth century by Francis James Child and still referred to by his name, while the recent reissue on CD of a number of recordings made during the mid-twentieth-century folk revival enables you to hear versions of some of them for yourself, including the treasury of Sussex songs preserved by the Copper family of Rottingdean and the Scottish songs and ballads of traveller singers such as Belle Stewart and the incomparable Jeannie Robertson. It is impossible to list all the available folk-tale collections from many lands and cultures, so I shall just draw your attention to Italo Calvino's wonderful *Fiabe italiane* (*Italian Folktales*),[14] which provided Italy in the twentieth century with a corpus of traditional tales comparable with Jacob and Wilhelm Grimm's famous nineteenth-century German folk-tale collection[15] and Charles Perrault's small but very important seventeenth-century French one,[16] which includes the tale of Cinderella, whose lost slipper was really made not of 'verre' (glass) but 'vair' (squirrel fur).

General knowledge

You will certainly need to know about:

> *The Encyclopaedia Britannica* (which you can also access on-line at
>   www.britannica.com)
> *Chambers's Encyclopaedia*
> *The Dictionary of National Biography*
> *The Times Atlas of the World*
> *Brewer's Dictionary of Phrase and Fable* (Millennium Edition)

Oxford University Press do a useful series of *Companions* to a wide range of subjects, including English literature and a number of foreign literatures, while Penguin publish dictionaries on subjects ranging from ancient history and architecture to science and saints.

Lavishly illustrated books on the prettier aspects of natural history exist in profusion. For a particularly useful series, which includes less appealing forms of wild life, such as toadstools, reptiles and spiders, as well as butterflies, birds, mammals, trees and flowers, I would recommend Collins' field guides and pocket guides.

You also need to know how human beings have used, and tried to understand, the natural world, so I would recommend the following:

Geoffrey Grigson, *Dictionary of English Plant Names* (Allen Lane, 1973)

Geoffrey Grigson, *The Englishman's Flora* (Dent, 1987)

Richard Mabey, *Flora Britannica* (Chatto and Windus, 1996)

John G. Vaughan and Catherine Geissler, *The New Oxford Book of Food Plants* (Oxford University Press, 1999)

T. H. White, *The Book of Beasts: Being a Translation from a Latin Bestiary of the Twelfth Century* (Cape, 1954)

History (including social history) is probably the most vital subject of all for the student of literature, and one in which merely consulting a few reference books is not enough. You need to do solid, sustained and structured reading, so find your way to the history section of your university library and discover what is available. (Making use of the title keyword and subject keyword search facilities of the on-line library catalogue should help you to locate the books you need.)

For pinning down the when and where of historical movements and events, you need Neville Williams's three-volume *Chronology of World History* (Helicon), plus Colin McEvedy's series of historical atlases, which include:

The New Penguin Atlas of Ancient History
The New Penguin Atlas of Medieval History
The Penguin Atlas of Modern History to 1815
The Penguin Atlas of Recent History: Europe since 1815
The Penguin Atlas of African History
The Penguin Atlas of North American History
The Penguin Historical Atlas of the Pacific
The New Penguin Atlas of Recent History

while *The Concise Oxford Chronology of English Literature* will help you to put texts into their historical contexts.

When venturing into unfamiliar fields of study, you may find it difficult to decide which authority is to be trusted. You may be able to consult a friend or a member of staff in another department. If not, it may help to compare the accounts of several different writers. Remember that information is not any the more trustworthy, nor theories any the more true, for appearing in print (let alone on the Web). Look carefully at the provenance of any material you might want to use, and try to develop the critical sense which will at least enable you to judge whether authors are serious and in good faith and whether their arguments are logical. This will also stand you in good stead when reading literary criticism. Finally, do not mistake coffee-table books for works of scholarship. Any book which calls itself *The Complete Book of X* or *All You Need to Know About Y* has been written for amateurs.

Trusting the author

One source of factual information which must be approached with caution is literature itself. Readers far too sophisticated to trust Milton's astronomy, or even his theology, often implicitly believe Shakespeare's version of medieval history and take all the Romantic poets (and not just John Clare, which would be reasonable) for experienced field naturalists. When great writers get their facts wrong, they often don't do it by halves. For example, in *To the Lighthouse* Virginia Woolf transports her childhood holiday home in St Ives, complete with its lush Cornish garden, to the Isle of Skye in the Scottish Highlands. Woolf did not actually set foot in Scotland until 1938, eleven years after the publication of her novel, when she found the real Isle of Skye 'remote as Samoa; deserted; prehistoric', and mythologized it as a place where 'Eagles are said to abound and often carry off sheep: sheep and Skye Terriers are the only industries; the old women live in round huts exactly the shape of skye terriers; and you can count all the natives on 20 feet',[17] which doesn't give one much faith in her regard for geographical accuracy.

A more doubtful case of error is Coleridge's *The Rime of the Ancient Mariner*, in which a dead albatross is hung as a penance around its killer's neck. If we think of this as the wandering albatross, *Diomedea exulans*, the thing is impossible since this requires the mariner to sustain the weight of a bird with a twelve- or thirteen-foot wing-span. However, John Livingston Lowes, in his classic study *The Road to Xanadu* (itself an object lesson in the art of looking things up), maintains that Coleridge may have been thinking instead of *Phoebetria palpebrata antarctica*, the so-called sooty albatross 'which is much the smaller bird' and 'might readily enough, as I know from experiment, have been carried suspended from a sailor's neck'[18] – testimony with which it is difficult to quarrel, but which I mention here to punch home the point that the best kind of research often involves getting as close to the writer's own source material as you can. For example, don't be content with some editor's précis of what Shakespeare cribbed his plots from but look up the very texts he read in Geoffrey Bullough's eight-volume *Narrative and Dramatic Sources of Shakespeare*.[19]

This is not to suggest that you should overlook the valuable work done by the editors of scholarly editions, who often provide the reader with a wealth of useful information in their introductions and footnotes. Indeed, you should make sure you don't handicap your own research by failing to make full use of the discoveries of previous researchers. Do remember, though, that you can often use them as the starting point for further discoveries of your own. Something as simple as actually reading the passage from Homer, Ovid or the Bible mentioned in a scholarly footnote can yield unexpected insights into the themes and details of a text.

Libraries and librarians

Since you cannot afford to own all the books on all the subjects you may want to investigate, you need to learn how to get the best out of libraries. People often suppose that a library is simply a collection of books under one roof, and that librarians are there to put the books back on the shelves. In fact, a library is a complex machine for storing and retrieving information. In addition, while the Web has only soulless search engines, every university library has an invaluable collection of librarians, each specializing in a different subject area. Librarians combine scholarly knowledge with expertise in information retrieval, and even the most exalted and professorial researchers need to make use of their skills. Provided you have a reasonably clear idea of what you are looking for, there should be a librarian who knows where, if anywhere, the information can be found.

Learning to use your university library's on-line catalogue enables you to discover (via relevant title and subject keywords) at least some of the books the library holds on the subjects you are interested in, but you will also need to familiarize yourself with the whereabouts of the various subject sections so that you can browse intelligently. Some of the books adjacent on the shelves to the ones you find in the catalogue may also be relevant to your research. In addition, your university library probably holds literature databases and other useful on-line resources, which it is well worth finding out about and familiarizing yourself with.

Searching on-line

In addition to looking for information in books and databases, you may also want to extend your researches deeper into cyberspace. Searching for information on the Web can be time-consuming and frustrating, but the following tips may help you to track down your quarry.

1: The simplest way to find information on the Web is via a search engine. The following section tells you how to search efficiently using Google, which at the moment is far and away the best search engine available. That may soon change, though, since Bill Gates's Microsoft empire is currently planning to launch its own search engine in an attempt to undermine Google. It's dog eat dog out there. Incidentally, another useful resource is Amazon, the on-line bookseller (www.amazon.com and www.amazon.co.uk) whose keyword search facility you can use to find, and sometimes get a glimpse inside, potentially interesting books which may well turn out to be in your university library or available via inter-library loan.

2: Be wary of anything you find on the Web, especially if there is no author name or academic address. It is often a good idea to search the websites of academic societies or other university departments, but remember that, while scholarly books and articles have to get past academic publishers, editors and referees, even apparently scholarly websites do not. This means that something written by someone at somewhere.ac.somewhere may well be the work of a monomaniac, a prankster, an undergraduate who knows less about the subject than you do, or just a fully paid-up member of that international coven, Women who Run With Virginia Wolves.[20] On the plus side, scholarly journals often have on-line index pages which you can find via Google, enabling you to source useful articles which you might not otherwise know about.

3: When searching, you need to choose keywords intelligently and imaginatively. If you discover that your keyword summons up far too many potential sites, a carefully chosen combination of keywords should help to narrow down the possibilities. However, you also need to exercise caution and common sense; rashly chosen keywords can all too easily lead you to 'hate' sites or porn sites.

4: If you often visit the same website, click the Refresh button each time you re-access it, as otherwise you will be given the old version stored in your computer's cache memory.

5: A word of warning to end with: searching the Web can be both time-wasting and addictive, so don't let yourself get caught up in the myth that it contains the answers to all problems. The information you need may well not be out there. Know when to give up and go back to the library.

Using Google

There are two types of search engine used to search the internet. Searchable subject indexes search over the titles and descriptions of sites, not the contents of individual pages. Yahoo! (www.yahoo.com) is an example of this type of index. Full-text search indexes, as their name suggests, search the full contents and titles of sites, and can therefore be used for much more focused searches than searchable subject indexes. Google (www.google.com, with a UK version at www.google.co.uk) is the most famous and comprehensive of these.

When you are searching only for a single keyword, the search engine knows exactly what you mean. The drawback is that you're likely to get a very large numbers of 'hits', since this is like looking for the specific quotation 'O my Luve's like a red, red rose' by looking up the word 'rose' in the index of the largest dictionary of quotations in the world. With enough time and patience, you'll find what you are looking for eventually, but only if you are prepared to sort through any number of sites devoted to such things as the American Rose Society and Henry VIII's warship the *Mary Rose*. Although some of these might lead you up interesting cul-de-sacs, unfocused web trawling of this kind is not so much a research method as a distraction mechanism for reluctant writers. It is much more sensible to refine or narrow your search by adding combinations of search terms, and Google offers you various short cuts for doing this.

It is a standard convention among computer scientists to distinguish text input into a computer terminal (or, as in this case, a Web page) from surrounding text by printing it in `Courier font` (since putting it in inverted commas might cause confusion over whether the quote marks were part of the input). I've adopted that convention here.

1: It's important to remember that Google has a limit of ten search terms — anything beyond that limit will be ignored in the search.

2: If you enter two or more search terms, Google's default behaviour is to assume that you actually want to search for *all* of them. In terms of its own algebraic language, it assumes that you have inserted an upper case AND between each of the search terms. So, the term `Shakespeare Hamlet` is read as `Shakespeare AND Hamlet`, and Google will return all pages which include both 'Shakespeare' and 'Hamlet' in them. Note that the keywords are treated as individual entities, so pages will be returned which include both of them, no matter how far apart they might be in the text.

3: If you want to indicate to Google that it should search for *either* or *any one* of your search terms, you need to use an upper case OR, like this:

`Shakespeare OR Hamlet`

It is important to remember to put AND and OR in capital letters, since otherwise, for reasons which will shortly become clear, Google will ignore them; but if you want to feel like a real techie, you can use the | ('pipe') character to represent OR:

`Shakespeare | Hamlet`

4: AND and OR can be combined for more refined searches. For example, if you want Google to search for one term and either of two others, you can use parentheses to indicate which of your terms is essential and which are alternatives. So the search

`Shakespeare (Hamlet | Othello)`

would return pages which included 'Shakespeare' and either 'Hamlet' or 'Othello' (not just those that contain both: that would be `Shakespeare Hamlet Othello`). If you want to specify that a particular keyword should definitely *not* be displayed in the results of your search, you should indicate this by prefixing the unwanted term with a minus sign (use the hyphen):

```
nightingale -florence
```

5: As I said earlier, Google treats individual keywords as single entities. If you are looking for a proper name, for example, and enter `Robert Burns`, the search engine will treat both names as separate terms and return pages where both appear, without regard to whether or not they appear together. Since Google is not case-sensitive (i.e. it makes no difference whether or not you use capital letters), your search will produce unwanted information about every hospital burns unit with a consultant called Robert. You can force Google to treat `robert burns` as a single search term by enclosing it in double quotation marks: `"robert burns"`. You should also use double quotation marks if you're searching for an actual quotation: the search term `"to be or not to be that is the question"`, for example, will certainly lead you to Hamlet's soliloquy, whereas `to be or not to be that is the question` will put you in touch with a lot of people wondering whether to blog or not to blog and to carpool or not to carpool.

6: Quotation marks are also useful if your search term contains one of Google's 'stop words'. 'Stop words' are words which occur very commonly in text and which Google habitually ignores, since to include them would lead to an unmanageable number of hits. Google's 'stop list' includes: a, about, are, at, by, from, I, in, of, how, that, the, this, to, will, who, what, where, when. You can force Google to search for stop words by enclosing them in quotation marks, or by putting plus signs in front of them. If you happened to be taking time off from researching your essay by looking for information about the pop band The Smiths, you would access fewer irrelevant sites by entering the search term `"the smiths"` or `+the smiths` than you would if you simply entered `the smiths`.

7: If your search term consists only of stop words, as it might if your displacement activity was looking for information on The Who, Google will treat them as though they aren't on the stop list, though it is likely that `"the who"` or `+the +who` would be a more product-ive search than `the who`.

8: After you've been Googling for a while, you'll realize that other words or phrases, though not formally on the Google stop list, are likely to return large numbers of pages. The key to successful Googling (i.e. not wasting a lot of time working your way through irrelevant material) is to get a feel for the way Google searches, and refine your search strings so that they're as snappy and relevant as possible. Our earlier example, `Shakespeare (Hamlet | Othello)`, for example, is likely to return millions of pages. The trick is to add extra keywords (up to the limit of ten), in the hope of refining the query to get something more useful. Lateral thinking is often needed here.

9: It is also worth remembering that Google now has country-specific sites. www.google.com tends to pull up results from the USA before those from overseas, so if, for example, you're looking for information about recent performances of Handel's opera *Semele* in London, England, it might be sensible to go to www.google.co.uk, type in the search string `Handel Semele London performances` and click the button to restrict your search to pages from the UK only.

10: One particularly useful Google trick for students of literature is the wildcard. Suppose that you are trying to locate a quotation, and can remember some of the words in the right order, but not all of them. In this case, you can substitute a wildcard for one or more words in your search string. Wildcards are represented by the asterisk symbol, and can stand *only* for full words, not (as in some other search engines) for parts of words: `"Methinks the la* doth pro-test too much"` would mean nothing to Google, but `"Methinks the * doth * too much"` might just get you the lady. Wildcards might also be useful in researching how particular words are used in a literary corpus. NB: wildcards do not count towards Google's ten-word limit, so they can also be used to get round it if necessary.

11: For more tips on how to use Google see Tara Calishain and Rael Dornfest, *Google Hacks* (O'Reilly and Associates, Sebastopol CA etc., 2003).

12: Google is an immensely powerful research tool, but it is also a drug which can take over your life and stop you ever doing any work again. Don't let it turn into a displacement activity when you have an essay deadline looming. Used creatively, Google can help to widen and deepen your research, but it can also be a source of bland or misguided literary criticism and inaccurate biographical information. Go carefully.

Serendipity

Finally, researchers surprisingly often find the answers to their questions through serendipity: the making of happy and unexpected discoveries by accident. The word was coined by the eighteenth-century gothic novelist Horace Walpole, inspired by the Persian fairy tale about the three princes of Serendip who 'were always making discoveries, by accident and sagacity, of things which they were not in quest of'.[21] The point about this kind of happy accident is that it seldom happens to the unprepared. If you search long and hard enough for gold you may discover a copper mine; if you bother to pick up the thing that sparkles by the side of the path it may be a diamond ring; but the person who never looks, whether carefully for something or alertly at everything, is unlikely to find anything at all.

Chapter 4

Essay topics

Choosing your own topic

When choosing your essay topic, there is only one rule. You should find an aspect of your subject in which you are keenly interested and write about that. Obviously you should not write about an Elizabethan author if you are taking a module on Victorian literature, or choose topics for a set of exam essays which will suggest to the examiners that you have read only one short novel and a handful of poems in the course of the term or semester; but, within the bounds of ordinary common sense, it should be your own interests which dictate what you write about. This does not mean choosing the easiest topic, or one you have already covered at A-level. On the contrary, it means developing a personal and imaginative response to the literature you read, being prepared to tackle large and difficult questions even if they sometimes defeat you, taking an original approach rather than a safe and conventional one. Anything which you write with real interest and enjoyment is likely to communicate that interest and enjoyment to the reader. The stock topic which bores you will bore your reader too.

Set topics and exam questions

When faced with a set topic, whether it takes the form of a question or a quotation, it is important to remember that there will be more than one possible way of handling it. You will often have been urged at school to 'make sure that you answer the question the examiners are asking', and indeed you should, but that does not mean that you should assume that the question contains its own built-in answer.

Let us suppose that, absurdly, you have been asked to tackle the famous exam question from that celebrated history book *1066 and*

All That: 'How can you be so numb and vague about Arabella Stuart?'[1] The examiners, even if they are Sellar and Yeatman, will not necessarily expect you to give a detailed account of the educational and social circumstances responsible for your lack of compassion for, and information about, poor Arabella, although (in so far as it illustrates the problem of what can be said to constitute 'history') that might not be a stupid answer. Nor is proving that you are not, in fact, numb and vague by giving a textbook account of her tragic life the only alternative open to you. You might, for instance, want to show that it was precisely the fact that, as an unmarried woman in the direct line of succession to the throne, Arabella might well have become historically significant which caused James I to go to such lengths to make sure that she remained obscure. Or again, since you are a student of literature, and literature is made out of words, you might want to argue that Arabella's fate and our indifference to it are alike contingent on the semantic gap between her first name (which, in its lack of a commonly accessible narrative context, signifies only the unknowable private self) and her fatal surname.[2]

With real, as with spoof, exam questions, there is no 'right' answer. Any carefully thought-out and cogently expressed answer is the right answer, provided it expresses a valid (and, if possible, honestly held) opinion on the subject.

The desert island essay

The desert island essay is the one you write after the shipwreck has deprived you of everything except a copy of the primary text. It tends to be an impoverished kind of essay. This is not to say that you should avoid writing an essay on a single text. Nor is it to say that when writing about Conrad's *Heart of Darkness* you should always put in a quotation or two from *Nostromo* to show that you have read that as well. Instead, you should cultivate a sense that novels and poems and plays do not exist all on their own, or simply in the context of their author's life and works, but are connected with the rest of literature, and with all the other arts, and with history and politics and religion and philosophy, and with the sciences, and with human life itself. The field of reference you can draw on is enormous. In practice, you will want to refer only to what is relevant to the subject in hand, but an imaginative sense of the possibilities open to you can transform your idea of what relevance means, and free you from the 'bare island'[3] and its solipsistic texts.

Chapter 5

Structure

Notes and drafts

The purpose of taking notes is to help you to remember things. It is not an especially virtuous activity in itself. Making notes indiscriminately on everything you read is a waste of time, and it is worse than a waste of time to take notes so assiduously during a lecture that you fail to take in what the lecturer is saying. Remember, too, when revising for exams, that reading your notes on someone else's book on *Paradise Lost* or *The Prelude* will leave you at two removes from the text. It is no substitute for rereading the poem itself, or at least some carefully chosen sections of it.

Some people find it helpful to make notes in the margins of books. This is all right provided the books belong to you. There is a special circle in hell reserved for people who write in library books.

You may also want to make notes of another kind, outlining the subject matter of your essay before you write it. It is generally supposed that the correct way to write an essay is to begin with notes, then to write a rough draft, and finally to rewrite the whole essay, polishing up the prose. Many people do work like this, but there is no point in making copious notes if you find that the exercise is more time-consuming than useful. Try the patent essay plan described in the following section instead. Nor is it necessary to write a rough draft unless you actually find it helpful. If you prefer to polish each sentence or paragraph as you go along, then do it like that. Above all, never start tinkering about with a perfectly satisfactory essay in the belief that because you wrote it easily it must be a first draft and not the thing itself.

Arguing a case

In order to argue a case, you need to have a case to argue. You cannot construct a well-argued essay by taking notes from half a dozen critical books and a lecture or two and then reconstituting those notes (suitably acknowledged) into a piece of continuous prose, and neither can you do it by simply sitting down and writing anything that comes into your head about the text in the order in which it occurs to you. Nor should your essay attempt to encompass the whole of a text. The project is both impossible and needless, since the text already encompasses the whole of itself. Instead of doing any of these things, you should find something that you want to say about the text – a discussion of its use of nature imagery; or of its response to the problem of evil; or of its satirical representation of polite society; or of the political significance of the conflict between its two central characters. Arguing your case will then be a question of arranging what you have to say in the order that makes it most effective. Think carefully about this before you start writing, but stay open to the possibility of changing the structure of the essay if new and interesting ideas occur to you while you are writing it.

The most efficient way of arranging your ideas into a well-argued case is to do the ordering on paper by constructing a detailed essay plan. There is more than one sensible way of doing this, but the method I am about to suggest has the merit of simplicity and doesn't involve drawing diagrams of spiders. However, I want to begin by warning you about two ways of making an essay plan which are positively counter-productive. The first is the method you may have been taught at school, based on the notion that every essay should include the same magic number of points or topics. This can be a neat way of generating the classic GCSE or A-level essay, which is precisely why it is no use to you now. The second is the plan which divides your essay into sections, each devoted to a vaguely defined theme described in half a page of labour-intensive but unfocused notes. Both of these methods are attempts to get the plan to do your thinking for you. With the Woolf patent essay plan, you do most of the thinking before you start making the plan. Here are the instructions:

1: Decide on your topic.

2: Do some solid and directed reading.

3: Do some equally solid and directed thinking, working out what you want to say in your essay. At this stage, it often helps to go for a long walk, taking a biro and a notebook in case you need to scribble down any brilliant ideas or phrases you might otherwise forget.

4: Take a large sheet of paper and jot down, in the order in which they occur to you, a brief reminder of each idea you have had, from major insights to the most minor points of detail. These reminders should not be in the form of whole paragraphs or even whole sentences. A short mnemonic phrase is all you need.

5: On a second large sheet of paper, arrange those short mnemonic phrases into clumps of related topics, then start arranging the clumps into a sequence. Keep on doing this, thinking about how you want your essay to begin and end and how best you can move from one point of the argument to another, until you have worried your collection of ideas into a sensible running order. You may well find, at this stage, that you have to discard one or two ideas which don't fit in, or think of a few new ones to plug gaps in your argument.

6: Make a list of your ideas in their final order, making sure that you leave a column of blank space for quotation references at the right hand side of the page.

7: Now think about what you are likely to want to quote to illustrate your ideas. Collect together the relevant books and locate all the quotations, inserting paper slips to mark the place. (Don't mark the actual pages or dog-ear their corners unless the books belong to you. Underlinings and marginal scribbles in library books make it much more difficult for other borrowers to scan the pages for the information they need.) As you find each quotation, add title keywords and page references, plus a brief indication of subject matter, opposite the relevant idea on your list.

8: You now have a detailed route map of the terrain to be covered by your essay and can concentrate on the actual writing. If you find that new and better ideas come into your head while you are writing, you will need to adapt the map to accommodate them.

Chapter 6

Writing

Style

> A style ought to make it easy for you to say all that you have to say, not, as most do, make it impossible for you to get free from one narrowed range of experience and expression.
>
> Randall Jarrell, *Poetry and the Age*

I want to begin with the story of a literary scandal which has quite a lot to tell us about style. In July 1943, the Australian symbolist poet Ern Malley died of Graves' disease at the age of twenty-five, still completely unknown and unpublished. After his death, his sister discovered his extraordinary collection of poems, *The Darkening Ecliptic*, and sent them to the editor of a small, experimental poetry magazine called *Angry Penguins*, which printed them along with a 'Preface and Statement' in which Malley talked about his poetic method:

> To discover the hidden fealty of certain arrangements of sound in a line and certain concatenations of the analytic emotions, is the 'secret' of style . . .
>
> Simplicity in our time is arrived at by an ambages. There is, at this moment, no such thing as a simple poem if what is meant by that is a point-to-point straight line relation of images. If I said that this was so because on the level where the world is mental occurrence a point-to-point relation is no longer genuine I shd be accused of mysticism. Yet it is so.[1]

The painter Sidney Nolan provided a cover illustration for the number of the magazine devoted to Malley's work. The poems raised a storm of controversy, which culminated in the prosecution for obscenity of

Max Harris, the young poet who edited *Angry Penguins*, whose own literary career was destroyed by his championing of Malley

Nowadays, Ern Malley is one of Australia's most famous poets, but supposing you had never heard of him and someone were to tell you that two words in the above account are bogus, which two would you pick? Almost certainly *Angry Penguins*, but despite the absurd title it was a real magazine with real aspirations to bring modernism to a reluctant Australian audience. Or you might plump for 'ambages' and 'ecliptic', but a glance at the *Shorter Oxford Dictionary* will tell you that ambages means 'roundabout or indirect modes of speech, for deceit, concealment, or delay', either in a literal or a figurative sense, while ecliptic means 'the great circle of the celestial sphere representing the sun's apparent path during a year'. The answer, of course, is that the two words are Ern Malley. He never existed. A couple of young army officers called James McAuley and Harold Stewart, poets themselves of a more conservative kind, spent a single afternoon (or so they claimed) inventing him, poems and preface and premature death and all, in a bid to prove that modernist poetry was tosh. If you reread the passage from Malley's Preface, you will see it actually claims that the 'secret' of his style is all in the sound, and that his poetic method is one of deceit and concealment. Argument still rages, though, especially in Australia, about whether McAuley and Stewart somehow managed to write real poetry by mistake.

The story of Ern Malley is salutary in two opposite ways. On the one hand, his poetry, hoax though it may have been, is so much more interesting than anything that his creators produced in their own right that his work is remembered while theirs is mostly forgotten. On the other hand, the Ern Malley affair shows that it is possible to use words to create a bogus persona, causing your own authentic voice to disappear in the process. If you choose to write in a grey and conventional way because it seems more scholarly not to obtrude your own personality into your prose, then you will be prevented from really communicating the excitement and the imaginative insights which should be a crucial part of your experience of literature, but, if you masquerade as the kind of fashionable critic whose work is clever-sounding but obscure, you will have acquired a set of mannerisms which may well prevent you from saying anything meaningful at all.

To William Cobbett, the secret of writing in an authentic voice was to forget about style and concentrate on the ideas you are trying to communicate: 'The *order* of the matter will be, in almost all cases, that of your thoughts. Sit down *to write what you have thought*, and not *to think what you shall write*.'[2] Doing this doesn't mean giving up the attempt to write interesting prose, since finding the best way to write down what you have thought may well involve considerable lateral thinking. On the contrary, it means recognizing that there is no one style which is uniquely suitable for literary criticism, and that the best possible style evolves from the effort to write as yourself. The following short list of essays will give you some idea of the possible scope and variety of critical prose, from the magisterial and scholarly to the quirky and outrageous. They are not offered as models to be copied but as examples of the value of refusing to copy, the value of allowing your prose to speak with an authentic and personal voice.

A. S. Byatt, 'Sylvia Plath: *Letters Home*', *Passions of the Mind* (Chatto and Windus, 1991)

Italo Calvino, 'The Odysseys within *The Odyssey*', *Why Read the Classics,* trans. Martin McLaughlin (Jonathan Cape, 1999)

Mary Carruthers, 'The Wife of Bath and the Painting of Lions', in *Feminist Readings in Middle English Literature*, ed. Ruth Evans and Lesley Johnson (Routledge, 1994)

Seamus Heaney, 'The Fire I' the Flint: Reflections on the Poetry of Gerard Manley Hopkins', *Preoccupations* (Faber, 1980)

Frank Kermode, 'Cornelius and Voltemand: Doubles in *Hamlet*', *Forms of Attention* (University of Chicago Press, 1985)

Cynthia Ozick, 'What Henry James Knew', *What Henry James Knew and Other Essays on Writers* (Jonathan Cape, 1993)

Camille Paglia, 'Tournament of Modern Personae: D. H. Lawrence's *Women in Love*', *Vamps & Tramps: New Essays* (Penguin, 1995)

Susan Sontag, 'Writing Itself: On Roland Barthes', *Where the Stress Falls* (Jonathan Cape, 2001)

At this point you may quite reasonably want to protest that you will have to begin by finding some examples of good writing to copy, even if only as a first stage towards the evolution of an individual voice. This will particularly be the case if your real problem is with a prose style which you were forced to adopt by the need to get good marks in school exams, the style of someone trying to cram in all the points which a conscientious teacher would be likely to reward with a tick in the margin. If you find yourself in need of a model, a good plain style for everyday, I would not advise you to look for it among literary critics, of whatever school or persuasion, though the best of them should expand your sense of the creative possibilities open to you. The style which I would recommend has nothing to do with literature at all, as you will see from the following book-list:

Philip Ball, *Bright Earth: The Invention of Colour* (Viking, 2001)

Richard Dawkins, *Unweaving the Rainbow: Science, Delusion and the Appetite for Wonder* (Penguin, 1998)

Robert Kaplan, *The Nothing That Is: A Natural History of Zero* (Allen Lane, 1999)

Tore Janson, *Speak: A Short History of Languages* (Oxford University Press, 2002)

Jonathan Miller, *On Reflection* (National Gallery Publications, 1998)

Anna Pavord, *The Tulip* (Bloomsbury, 1999)

Matthew Sweet, *Inventing the Victorians* (Faber, 2001)

Frances Wood, *Did Marco Polo Go to China?* (Secker and Warburg, 1995)

What these authors have in common is that they are all experts explaining to the intelligent lay reader, or at any rate in language the intelligent lay reader can understand, a complex subject in which they are deeply interested. The problems involved in doing this are similar even though their fields of expertise range from art to exploration, and from social and cultural history to the histories of science, mathematics and gardening, and this leads them to write prose with similar kinds of virtues. These writers have large vocabularies and use technical terms with precision, but otherwise they write in a plain but shapely version of the language of everyday. They employ a wide range of reference and quotation (often from quite diverse fields) if this can illustrate the subject, but never irrelevantly. Above all, they are aware that, if the reader is to keep a clear and logical grasp of the complexities of the subject, the organization of the argument must itself be clear and logical throughout.

Style here becomes a matter of more than surface polish: the book must be written in such a way if its subject is to be understood; and yet these books (all seriously good and interesting ones and well worth reading for their own sakes) all clearly bear the marks of their authors' personalities. Those marks have been impressed on the prose in the self-forgetful process of making, as the marks of the potter's hands are impressed on a pot. It is hard for literary critics, writing, as they do, about writing, to be self-forgetful in this way, but for them too style is more than a matter of surface polish. If you express an idea in a slightly different way it becomes a slightly different idea. What we say and how we say it are not in the end separable from one another.

You will notice that there is an apparent inconsistency here: I began by urging you to write in an individual way and I have ended by praising self-forgetfulness. This inconsistency is the paradox that lies at the root of all criticism, one that our current culture of literacy tests and exams can all too easily cause us to forget. The true purpose of criticism is not to demonstrate the cleverness of the critic but to cast light on the text and its contexts. That light may well come from an unexpected angle and cause the reader to perceive the text in a new and different way, but the critic who interposes his or her own cleverness between the reader and the text is likely to prove a source not of illumination but obscurity. W. H. Auden expressed this perfectly in his essay on 'Reading' in *The Dyer's Hand*:

> A poet or a novelist has to learn to be humble in the face of his subject matter which is life in general. But the subject matter of a critic, before which he has to learn to be humble, is made up of authors, that is to say, of human individuals, and this kind of humility is much more difficult to acquire.[3]

However, there is another kind of humility which the student essay-writer must take pains to shake off – the humility of the pupil obediently regurgitating knowledge. When you write an essay, you too become an expert explaining a complex subject in which you are deeply interested, and your tutor, reading that essay, becomes a student. The examiner who awards you high or low marks for that essay is responding not to what you have learnt but to what you can teach. The real reason for learning to write in your own voice is because there is a reader out there who does not yet know what you have to say, and who wants to hear it.

Words, plain and lacy

There used to be a firm of Brighton solicitors called Plane and Lacey. It is probable that the clients of that firm expected to get the same kind of service from both partners, and so, no doubt, they did; but writers who expect to get the same kind of service from the lacy words as they do from the plain ones are likely to find themselves badly deceived, particularly if they pick the words by ear. Acting on the principle that a word that sounds the same only fancier must also mean the same only fancier, these unfortunate writers say 'fortuitous' when they mean fortunate, and 'longevity' when they mean length, and 'emasculated' when they mean manly, and so are altogether brought to resemble that famous Mrs Malaprop who boasted of her 'nice derangement of epitaphs'.[4]

The cure for this unhappy tendency is to keep a dictionary to hand and use it to check up on the meaning of any word about which you have the faintest doubt. Some random checks among the words of which you think you are certain will help you to estimate the extent of the problem.

A more subtle version of the plain and lacy fallacy is seen in those writers who believe that long and abstract words and phrases are always better – more meaningful, more learned, more effective – than short and concrete ones. Deluded by the belief that it is possible to translate plain words into lacy ones without changing the nuances of what is being said, they are in danger of sounding at best pompous, at worst inhuman. Compare the following statements:

> Fanny Price approaches maturation in a non-affective and inadequately supportive familial environment.

> Fanny Price grows up in a family unable either to sympathize with her or to love her.

An excellent, if old-fashioned, antidote to this particular form of lacy language is Ernest Gowers' *The Complete Plain Words*.[5] This was written primarily for civil servants, but if your problem is that you write like a civil servant (or a sociologist, or a psychiatric social worker) you may well find it worth reading.

A third, and less severe, form of lacy language afflicts those writers who feel the need to draw a kindly veil over strong words. Such a writer will say that 'Hamlet feels himself *almost* polluted by his mother's incest', and that 'Hopkins, in the Terrible Sonnets, expresses *something nearly approaching* religious despair'. The cure for this is to notice that you are doing it.

The above is all advice about how not to choose words; how, then, are you to choose them? Not, obviously, by applying the flip-side of the above rules and confining yourself to short, concrete, unqualified phrases. Words should be chosen for their exactness, but the exactness of a word depends on its context. People often think of words, and try to use them, as if they invariably carried the same fixed face-value of meaning. In fact, words, and particularly what we think of as simple words, often have a surprisingly rich, subtle and varied range of past and current meanings, as you can easily confirm by looking up a few 'simple' words – grain, green, kind, nature, stout – in the *Oxford English Dictionary*. In use, the meaning of a word is defined by its context, but words also have a penumbra made up of our memories of all the other possible contexts in which we might expect to find them. Poets often make use of this penumbra – Milton's shoals of fish that 'glide under the green wave'[6] seem beautiful and exciting to us for exactly this reason – and so can the essay-writer who is properly alive to the nuances of words in all their combinations. However, this tendency of words to change colour and mean more than we meant them to mean can also lead the writer into difficulties.

Words are generated by human needs and experiences, gain or lose meanings as human societies alter, but they refuse to be coerced by individuals. Lewis Carroll's Humpty Dumpty, who thought he could be their master – 'Impenetrability! That's what *I* say!'[7] – not surprisingly ended up in pieces. The training of ear and eye which enables you to use words with precision is not something which can be achieved overnight, but everything that you write or read with proper attention to the language is a means towards it. Remember, too, that the work of literature is itself part of the context of the words written about it. The first of my two sentences about Fanny Price is made absurd by the presence of Fanny. Replace her by 'the typical under-age offender' and the sentence, although still jargon, is no longer ridiculous; but equally it no longer refers to Jane Austen.

Jargon and theory-speak

Jargon is a word with a cluster of related meanings. It can be the twittering of birds, a babel of sounds, a debased and hybrid language, a cipher, or simply gibberish, and all but the first of these could apply to the writing of essays. However, the kind of jargon I want to consider here is technical language. The *OED* says that the word is 'applied contemptuously to any mode of speech abounding in unfamiliar terms, or peculiar to a particular set of persons, as the language of scholars or philosophers, the terminology of a science or art'. The people who apply the term contemptuously are presumably those who cannot decode this particular jargon, the outsiders. Students are often perplexed about whether, and in what ways, they should be using jargon of this sort.

Obviously you cannot avoid technical language altogether. Literary criticism has its own technical terms (see J. A. Cuddon's *The Penguin Dictionary of Literary Terms and Literary Theory* if you want to find out more about them) and so do all those other disciplines which have an important bearing on literature. If you want to look at Shakespeare's *Hamlet* in the light of psychoanalysis, or at Nathaniel Hawthorne's *The Scarlet Letter* in the light of semiotics, or at T. S. Eliot's *Four Quartets* in the light of Einstein's theory of relativity, you cannot do so without recourse to technical language. However, it is as well to remember that, while scholars adopt special terminologies in order to be exact about things which the language is vague about, they also use them to confirm their status as insiders, and this is a use of jargon which limits understanding and can sometimes prevent it altogether. This is something which you particularly need to bear in mind if you develop an interest in literary theory.

For the uninitiated, literary theory is not a theory about how literature should be written or read or studied. Indeed, it isn't a single, unified theory at all, but rather a loose assemblage of different, often conflicting, theoretical approaches, drawn from a wide range of disciplines (especially linguistics, anthropology, philosophy, political theory and psychoanalysis) all of which offer ways of focusing on the formal properties which equate literary texts with the totality of other communication systems and cultural codes. In fact, literary theory is the antithesis of the kind of old-fashioned literary criticism which concerned itself with the beauty, morality, social relevance or life-enhancing qualities of poems, plays and novels, since it offers a host of ways of dispensing with the idea that literature is aesthetically priviliged or uniquely able to map itself on to reality – if indeed, given that it is only through coded systems we are able to perceive the world, reality can really be said to exist.

All this can seem off-puttingly abstract, depriving the man in the street, not to mention the woman in the boardroom, operating theatre or pulpit, of an informed understanding of what is going on in the world of literary studies. It can also involve a reflexive or regressive concern with meta-languages (languages about language) which sometimes make the post-structuralist or semiotician appear trapped in a linguistic hall of mirrors. On the plus side, and whether or not Terry Eagleton is being premature in announcing the death of 'high theory'[8] (the austerely intellectual kind which obliges you to wrestle with the work of Michel Foucault or Jacques Lacan), the influence of literary theory has had a freeing and broadening influence on the work done, even by non-theorists, in departments of English and foreign literature. To start with, it has injected a needed intellectual rigour into literary studies, putting paid to the idea that reading literature is a culturally sanctioned form of escapism or a soft focus version of ethics. It has broadened the scope of what can be studied, ending the exclusive preoccupation with 'great' works of literature at the expense of historically or socially significant genres and texts which, for whatever reason, failed to make it into the canon, and also breaking down the barriers between literature and other academic disciplines. Above all, it has foregrounded the idea of the author as at least in part the voice of his or her cultural context, fostering a new realization of the part the reader plays in 'performing' the text.

However, it remains the case that literary theory can cause linguistic problems for the student essay writer, though these are only partly to do with the use of technical terms. As Jonathan Culler points out in his useful little book *Literary Theory: A Very Short Introduction*, 'Theory is a bunch of (mostly foreign) names; it means Jacques Derrida, Michel Foucault, Luce Irigaray, Jacques Lacan, Judith Butler, Louis Althusser, Gayatri Spivak, for instance.'[9] Unfortunately, all too often this has meant that texts which, in their own language, are excitingly (if sometimes also dauntingly) experimental have been translated into that unwieldy and inelegant form of English known as translatorese, helping to create a transatlantic critical meta-language which can be described only by quoting Randall Jarrell's prophetic simile:

> if the two bears that ate the forty-two little children who said to Elisha, 'Go up, thou baldhead' – if they, after getting their Ph.D.'s from the University of Göttingen, had retired to Atta Troll's Castle and written a book called *A Prolegomena to Every Future Criticism of Finnegans Wake*, they might have written so.[10]

Not for nothing does the old Italian proverb tell us that 'translator' equals 'traitor'.[11] One excellent reason for starting your exploration of the 'brave new world'[12] of theory with Culler's lucid introduction is that it demonstrates by example that it is not actually necessary for a theorist to sound like a bad 1960s translation from the French.

A very different, and much more immediately engaging, type of theoretical writing (to be found, for example, in gender studies and queer theory) involves a kind of serious and creative playfulness with language. This playfulness can also include borrowing terminology from a number of different boxes, as Karen Hodder points out:

> Students need to be aware that technical language is often a cocktail of professional discourses, e.g. gender theory tends to borrow (sometimes randomly, one feels) from sociology, psychology and scientific theory (as in all the current talk about 'sperm wars'). Novices can often lack awareness of where jargon is coming from, or that its many varieties are not always distinct from one another, even in a single text.[13]

Your own experiments with language may not all be successful, at any rate to begin with, but it is important to remember that you should be trying to stretch the possible ways of conveying meaning, not just indulging in *exercices de style*. This means making sure that you are quite clear about the meaning both of the ideas and of the technical terms which you use in your essay, and doing your best to write in such a way that your reader also understands them. Ben Jonson's wise advice applies with particular force when the ideas being discussed are already difficult in themselves:

> Whatsoever loseth the grace, and clearness, converts into a riddle; the obscurity is marked, but not the value . . . Our style should be like a skein of silk, to be carried, and found by the right thread, not ravelled, and perplexed; then all is a knot, a heap.[14]

You should remember, too, that not all of the major cultural figures whose work continues to offer fruitful metaphors and methodologies for literary studies are still perceived as being at the cutting edge in their own disciplines. Few historians now believe uncritically in the Marxist dialectic. Many psychologists have become radically sceptical about Freud. Being able to place such figures in the history of ideas is important too.

Above all, you should never pack your essay (or, indeed, your seminar presentation) full of impressive-sounding but incomprehensible theory-speak in the hope that, even if *you* don't understand it, your audience will. To do that is to reduce your prose to a babel of sounds, a debased and hybrid language, a cipher, or simply gibberish.

Slips and solecisms

> Total and sudden transformations of a language seldom happen; conquests and migrations are now very rare: but there are other causes of change, which, though slow in their operation, and invisible in their progress, are perhaps as much superior to human resistance, as the revolutions of the sky, or intumescence of the tide.[15]

As Samuel Johnson points out, words change their meanings over time. Sometimes this is to accommodate technological innovations: as fewer of us work with axes and mattocks and more of us work with computers, a hacker has ceased to be primarily someone who roughly cuts or chops. Sometimes it is in response to social change: for the Victorians, a snob was a social climber, but, when despicable social climbing was transformed into admirable upward social mobility, the word 'snob' began instead to describe a person who looks down on others on class grounds. Sometimes the change is simply down to human nature: the word 'presently' used to mean 'straight away', and it isn't too hard to work out why it now means 'in a little while'. However, the real problem for serious writers, including academic ones, is that a major way in which language changes over time is through the standardization of variant forms – what purists like to think of as errors. Johnson, who knew that this process is unstoppable since 'sounds are too volatile and subtle for legal restraints',[16] comments sadly:

> pronunciation will be varied by levity or ignorance, and the pen must at length comply with the tongue; illiterate writers will at one time or other, by publick infatuation, rise into renown, who, not knowing the original import of words, will use them with colloquial licentiousness, confound distinction, and forget propriety.[17]

Apart from a small class of onomatopoeic words which actually imitate the things they signify – such as 'splat', 'curlew', 'sussuration' – there is no logical connection between the sound of a word and its meaning, though there are historical reasons why we use the words we do. Since the meanings of words are simply the meanings their users attach to them, once malapropisms become sufficiently widespread they cease to be mistakes; but this inevitably leaves a grey area in which confusion abounds. 'Flaunt' begins to take on the meanings of flout, but not vice versa. 'Prevaricate' more and more commonly stands in for 'procrastinate', but its original meaning is not yet extinct and may well revive. Since scholarly discourse needs to be precise, it is important to try to avoid those solecisms which have not yet established themselves as a new orthodoxy. Though the following glossary is by no means exhaustive, it does give you a sense of what to beware of.

actress   See *poetess*.

affect/effect   If something affects you, it has an effect on you – not vice versa. 'Affect' as a noun is sometimes used by psychologists and psychoanalysts, but to mean a mood or emotion, not a result or consequence.

ancestors   See *antecedents*.

antecedents / ancestors   Your ancestors are your foremothers and forefathers; your antecedents (in the plural) are the details of your past history. 'Antecedent' can also mean something which precedes something else, especially in logic or grammar, and can be used as an adjective as well as a noun.

as / like   It is a common mistake to use 'like' when you really mean 'as' or 'as if'. Compare the following examples:

It is almost like the movement of Lily's brush across the canvas parallels that of Mr Ramsay's boat as it sails across the bay to the Lighthouse.

It is almost as if the movement of Lily's brush across the canvas parallels that of Mr Ramsay's boat as it sails across the bay to the Lighthouse.

behalf   If something is done on your behalf it is done *for* you *by* someone else.

blatantly   If something is blatant, it is obtrusive or conspicuous, probably in a loud or vulgar way; so you can't use 'blatantly' as a synonym for 'very' or 'extremely' in contexts where the quality being highlighted is a positive or neutral one. Jane Austen's prose is not blatantly witty.

demise 'Demise' means death, downfall or disappearance – something disastrous and final.

disinterested If you are disinterested, the kind of interest you don't have is the kind that Members of Parliament are required to declare, so a disinterested witness is an impartial one.

effect See *affect*.

enormity While it is no longer actually incorrect to talk about the enormity of something when you mean that it is very large, it can be misleading to do so because enormity also means a terrible crime or shocking outrage. 'The enormity of the success of Harry Potter' might suggest to your reader not that J. K. Rowling has sold a lot of books but that you think it outrageous that people have bought them. Try 'scale' or 'magnitude' instead.

fine-tooth comb A fine-tooth comb is a comb with narrow, closely spaced teeth. Mothers go through their children's hair with a fine-tooth comb after an outbreak of nits in the primary school, and researchers go through their data with a fine-tooth comb looking for bugs of a different kind. There is no such thing as a tooth-comb, whether fine or otherwise.

flaunt / flout To flaunt is to peacock about, to show off oneself or one's possessions. If you've got it, flaunt it. Nowadays it is also sometimes used in place of flout: to disregard the rules or to express contempt for someone or something – but this can lead to misunderstanding. 'She flaunted the regulations' might suggest that she flourished the rulebook like a demonstrative traffic warden.

flout See *flaunt*.

fortuitous / fortunate If something is fortuitous, it happens by chance or luck. The optimistic idea that all luck is good luck has led to its being wrongly taken to mean fortunate.

fortunate See *fortuitous*.

free rein   If a horse is given free rein, it is given its head, allowed to run freely without restraint from its rider. The saying has nothing to do with royalty. The Queen may be 'long to reign over us' but she doesn't have free rein to run the country.

fulsome   Fulsome praise is lavish and effusive and probably overdone.

imply / infer   To imply something is to hint or suggest it rather than to say it directly. To infer something is to deduce or conclude it. You infer from what I imply.

incredibly   means 'unbelievably'. In colloquial English it is often used to mean 'very' or 'extremely', but in a piece of academic prose this usage makes the writer sound gushing and naive. So avoid.

infamous   means shamefully evil or vile. An infamous person is famous, if at all, for being wicked, and thus deserving of infamy.

infer   See *imply*.

lead / led   The past tense of the verb to lead is spelt 'led'. People get confused about this because there are also two different nouns which are both spelt lead, and one of them, the base metal from which coffins used to be made, rhymes with the past tense of the verb to lead. So remember the poet's mournful words to the nightingale:

> King Pandion he is dead,
> All thy friends are lapp'd in lead.[18]

Dead: lead – it's easy. This is the only kind of lead pronounced with a short vowel; the other noun spelt in the same way means the clue by which the sleuth is led to the killer's identity, or the strap you attach to a dog's collar before leading it, or being led by it, for a companionable stroll.

like   See *as*.

literally   In informal writing or speech, 'literally' usually prefaces an exaggerated account rather than a strictly accurate one: 'she literally turned green with envy'. In formal writing, if something happens literally, it happens exactly as described.

niece is so spelt. People get it wrong because they hazily remember the rule *i* before *e* except after *c*. After *c*, yes, but not before it.

notorious means well-known, usually in the pejorative sense of having a bad reputation. During their lifetimes, Byron was a notorious poet while Tennyson was a famous one.

one-dimensional Mathematically speaking, a sphere is three-dimensional, a circle is two dimensional, while only a point or a straight line is one-dimensional – and if you have two straight lines at an angle to each other, you are already into two dimensions. So a flatly drawn or deliberately stylized character can be described as two-dimensional, but only a character as resolutely off-stage and unexplained as Samuel Beckett's Godot can be described as one-dimensional.

playwright The old English word 'wright' meant a craftsman, so a playwright is someone who *makes* plays (not someone who writes them), just as a wheelwright is someone who makes wheels.

poetess / actress Poets who happen to be women have always been insulted by the word 'poetess', and nowadays actors who happen to be women often feel the same way about the word 'actress'. When the medical establishment first lifted its ban on women qualifying as doctors, there was an attempt to saddle the new GPs with the patronising title of doctrix, but fortunately it didn't catch on.

practice (*noun*) / practise (*verb*) Just that – but note the analogy with prophecy / prophesy.

practise See *practice*.

prevaricate / procrastinate It is a very common mistake – in the editorial columns of broadsheet newspapers as well as in student essays – to write 'prevaricate' when what is actually meant is 'procrastinate', but it is a mistake which could land the editor, if not the student essay-writer, in the libel court. To prevaricate, which derives from the Latin word *varus* (bent or crooked, or even knock-kneed), means to speak or behave in a deceptive or devious way – in other words, to be a liar or a cheat. To procrastinate, which derives from the Latin word *cras* (tomorrow) means to delay or put off doing something. If you fail to hand in your essay on time, you are procrastinating. If you pretend that the dog ate your essay, you are prevaricating.

procrastinate   See *prevaricate*.

prophecy (*noun*) / prophesy (*verb*)   A prophet is someone who prophesies, not someone who prophesizes – and you prophesy by uttering prophecies, or perhaps just a single prophecy.

prophesy   See *prophecy*.

quote is a verb, 'quotation' is a noun.

religiosity can mean religious belief, but to talk about someone's religiosity can be ambiguous, since you might mean not that they were religious but that they were religiose: excessively or even hypocritically pious. It is probably safer to restrict religiosity to its more common meaning of exaggerated or plaster saintly piety, and use religiousness as the abstract noun derived from religious.

sea change   In Shakespeare's *Tempest*, when Ariel sings, 'Full fathom five thy father lies,' the 'sea change' which turns dead men's bones into coral is not a considerable change or a step change (whatever that may be) but a transformation caused by the sea. It is not too late for 'sea change' as used by journalists and politicians to go out of fashion, provided you help to preserve one of Shakespeare's most magical songs by resolving never to use this particular cliché.

simile   The plural is 'similes', not 'similies'.

simplistic means oversimplified, much too simple, affectedly simple. It doesn't simply mean simple.

state   'Camille Paglia states' doesn't mean the same thing as 'Camille Paglia says'. To state something is to give a clear, reasoned account of it, usually in the belief that what is being stated is objectively true. Camille Paglia may instead be arguing, suggesting, claiming, implying, asserting – in fact, she usually is.

torturous   See *tortuous*.

tortuous / torturous   'Tortuous' derives from the Latin word *tortuosus* (full of turns and windings) and means precisely that, either literally, as in the case of a mountain track, or metaphorically, in the sense of indirect or devious. Unlike 'torturous', which means agonizingly painful or tormenting, it has nothing to do with the word 'torture'.

underestimate   People often say 'it is impossible to underestimate' when they actually mean the opposite. If it is impossible to underestimate something then no estimate you can form of it could possibly be too low.

weaved / wove   Oddly enough, there are two different, though related, verbs to weave. The one which means to thread your way through obstacles or to sway from side to side takes the past tense 'weaved', while the one which means to interlace threads into a fabric takes the past tense 'wove'. So, the Artful Dodger weaved through the crowd, but the Lady of Shalott wove her web.

wherefore   means why – hence the saying 'the whys and the wherefores'. When Juliet on her balcony asks, 'Wherefore art thou Romeo?' she is wishing he belonged to a different family and thus had a different name, not wondering why he hasn't showed up. But of course you already knew that.

Mixing your metaphors

To start with, what is a metaphor in its unmixed state? Metaphor, along with its close cousin simile, is the most important and widespread of figures of speech. In my schooldays we were taught to chant, 'simile is the figure of speech in which one thing is *compared* to another which it resembles only in one respect', whereas metaphor, which can be thought of as a condensed simile, is 'the figure of speech in which one thing is *identified* with another which it resembles only in one respect.' Some examples will help to bring these arid formulae to life. When Herrick says of his own relationship with God,

> Lord, I am like a Misletoe,
> Which has no root, and cannot grow,
> Or prosper, but by that same tree
> It clings about; so I by thee,[19]

he is using a simile. When Emily Dickinson says of the snow,

> It sifts from Leaden Sieves –
> It powders all the Wood.
> It fills with Alabaster Wool
> The Wrinkles of the Road –[20]

she is using metaphors. You will see that metaphor, with its power to transform the commonplace, is the stronger and more magical of these figures. Simile asks us a riddle – why is a girl on her wedding day like a swan? – but metaphor, like that much older kind of riddle which was also a spell, transforms the girl into a swan before our very eyes.

A mixed metaphor is what happens when you apply two or more incongruous metaphors to the same object. The reason for avoiding mixed metaphors is not that they are incorrect but that they are powerfully and magically able to make their perpetrators look silly. Sometimes mixed metaphors can be the unhappy union of a couple of happy thoughts. The writer who described Emerson as 'an abandoned cul-de-sac stranded on a deserted beach' at least produced a striking image, a blind alley amazingly altered

> So that it seems a thing endued with sense:
> Like a sea-beast crawled forth, that on a shelf
> Of rock or sand reposeth, there to sun itself.[21]

More often the mixed metaphor is the result of muddled thinking and a failure to notice that the words being used are figurative ones. The next two examples both illustrate this, though the writer of the first one may have been thinking in a hazy way about ships.

> Chaucer's humour is complex and merely employs the benign tack as a vehicle to pursue the end products.

> The atmosphere in which the entire play is steeped is engraved into the collective minds of the audience with the very first scene.

Beware, too, of the sentence with a second and unintended meaning: 'Arcadian pastoral makes no attempt at realism; the shepherds seem to spend all day just folding and unfolding their sheep.'

It is worth remembering that this kind of ambiguity can arise simply from the misplacing of one of the elements of a sentence. Imagine the cries of 'Why not today?' which must have greeted this example from *The Guardian*:

> The Liberal Democrats voted overwhelmingly for a change in the law to recognize gay partnerships yesterday.[22]

It is also worth remembering that a national tradition of satire and one-liners makes English (unlike French) a tricky language in which to indulge in solemnly meaningful puns and portentous double entendres, though a good one in which to punch home a point with wit and verve. The Monty Python team may have disbanded but they cast a long shadow.

It is fair to say that your academic reader will enjoy your mixed metaphors and other verbal clangers (some even collect them, hence the real-life examples above) but it is an enjoyment which makes it harder for the reader to take your ideas seriously. The best way to avoid mixed metaphors is to get into the habit of reading carefully through your essay before you hand it in. In obstinate cases it helps to read the essay aloud. Anything which sounds absurd is likely to seem just as absurd to the reader; anything which sounds unnatural or contorted is likely to strike the reader in just the same way.

How to quote

There are many good reasons for using quotations in your essays. Quotations provide an economical way of clinching the points in an argument; they can draw attention to unexpected beauties, flaws or inconsistencies in the work you are discussing; and they restore to the reader, who may last have read it some time ago, a live sense of the language of the text. In addition, they can be delightful in themselves, like those pictures and conversations without which Carroll's Alice thought no book worth reading.[23]

Students often wonder if there is a rule about how much you should quote. The answer is that you should quote what will best serve to illuminate your point, neither more nor less. Sometimes a single sentence, or a single line of verse, will be enough; sometimes you will need a whole paragraph or a whole sonnet. When quoting, you must take care to pick precisely the right passage. Neither the random chunk of text with the image you want to draw attention to buried somewhere inside it, nor the stray line which may perhaps remind the reader of the relevant couplet you fail to quote, will make your point effectively. You must be careful, too, not to quote in such a way that you distort your author's meaning. It is sensible to avoid the really obvious quotation, which may be a jewel of our literature in its proper place, but in the context of your essay will strike the reader as a cliché.

Having chosen your quotation, you must darn it neatly into the syntax of your essay. People who never make gross grammatical errors in their own prose often feel quite happy to write things like this:

> Appalled at his delay in avenging his father's murder, Hamlet feels himself to be, 'O, what a rogue and peasant slave am I!'

The quotations in this kind of writing stand out like undigested lumps in the neck of an ostrich. Since Shakespeare's words cannot be rewritten to suit the exigencies of the essay-writer's prose, some alteration must be made either in the precise passage chosen or in the sentence which contains it:

> Appalled at his delay in avenging his father's murder, Hamlet feels himself to be 'a rogue and peasant slave'.

> Appalled at his delay in avenging his father's murder, Hamlet exclaims, 'O, what a rogue and peasant slave am I!'

In order to let the reader know when you are quoting, short quotations should be enclosed in inverted commas while longer ones should be indented and separated from your own prose by line spaces. The section on 'Footnotes and bibliographies' in Chapter 10 tells you how to acknowledge the sources of your quotations. It is particularly important to be scrupulous about this when you are quoting from secondary material. No one is going to think that you have invented a few well-known lines by Keats, but you could easily appear to be claiming authorship of the opinions of some unidentified critic of Keats if you quote those opinions without due acknowledgement.

When quoting from criticism, it is important to remember that the fact that something has been printed doesn't prove it to be true (still less the fact that someone has bothered to put it on the Web). Nor is there much point in copying out dull or obvious remarks simply because they were made by some famous professor. Quotations from critics need to be chosen just as carefully as quotations from the text.

How not to give offence

All writers of scholarly prose need to give careful thought to the way they handle such issues as race, gender, creed and orientation, not in order to present an appearance of political correctness but because scholarly writing, like any other kind of writing, can easily cause real hurt or offence to its readers. The fact that those readers are your tutors or examiners may make you feel that they are somehow impervious to such concerns, a misapprehension which may be compounded by the way that some kinds of academic discourse deliberately flirt with the outrageous as a means of uncovering and exploring hidden social subtexts. But it is important to remember that, while it is open to anyone to avoid reading a book or an article which they know is likely to offend them, university teachers cannot refuse to read their students' essays. The issue is further complicated by the understandable tendency to allow greater latitude in the matter of potentially offensive language to members of historically oppressed or disadvantaged groups. However great the temptation, the language of the barricades is best avoided in academic discourse, not only because social justice cuts both ways – men can't help having been born with a Y chromosome; straight people are entitled to their orientation too; no one is guilty of their ethnicity – but also because the kind of empathy which enables you to discuss difficult subject matter without either avoiding the issues involved or causing unnecessary hurt is closely related to the sensitivity to the implications of language which allows you to judge tone and register in your study of literature.

One thing which can make this sort of tact more difficult is the fact that many of the writers of the past held views or used expressions which would nowadays be considered unacceptable. Joseph Conrad, in *Heart of Darkness*, has his narrator Marlow refer to the enslaved and exploited inhabitants of the Congo as 'savages'. While Conrad is, of course, being ironic here – the many acts of savagery in the story are all performed or instigated by Europeans – this is not a term which a present-day Conrad would feel able to use in this way, so you need to be careful, when writing your essay on Conrad, to make sure that you don't slip into using it uncritically yourself. You also need to give some thought to the related problem of how to place and judge texts like this. To what extent are writers culpable for sharing views widely held in the periods and societies in which they wrote? Should you see Conrad as an imperialist writer whose apparently anti-colonial agenda in *Heart of Darkness* can easily be unmasked by attentive reading, or should you try to read his tale in the light of its historical context and argue that, having chosen to settle and make his career as a writer in late nineteenth-century Britain, it is not surprising that he saw the local brutality, rather than the sheer brute fact, of colonialism as the problem? After all, his friend Rudyard Kipling's description of the British Empire's governing role as 'the White Man's burden' was still so deeply entrenched half a century later that British opponents of that very idea campaigned under the slogan 'self-government is better than good government'. In Conrad's case there are strong arguments on both sides of the debate, with the critic Edward Said brilliantly playing the part of counsel for the prosecution;[24] whichever line you take, you need to be aware of the opposing case.

On the other hand, it is important to be attentive enough to the ways in which language changes over time to be able to recognize when it is not a writer's ideology but simply his or her vocabulary which may be a source of misunderstanding for the present-day reader. Even in a culture highly sensitized to the issue, the attempt to use non-denigratory language can lead to successive shifts in usage as each carefully neutral and inoffensive term is hijacked by the prejudiced, a process sometimes made more complicated by the reclaiming and ironizing of abusive language by the very people it was originally aimed at. In Henry James's novels, the word 'queer' simply meant odd or strange; the first citation in the *Oxford English Dictionary* of its use as a derogatory synonym for homosexual is dated 1922. 'Homosexual' itself was seen as a neutral term until the word 'gay' moved from slang to mainstream usage, providing a much-needed everyday, non-medicalized word for same-sex orientation. This in turn led to some opposition from purists who regretted the loss of the word in its original sense of lighthearted or carefree (Yeats's poem *Lapis Lazuli* was one of the casualties of this) as well as from less well-intentioned critics who maintained that, since homosexuals were by definition unhappy, the word 'gay' was obviously a misnomer. Since then, the word 'queer' has been reclaimed by queer theorists but is still often used as a term of abuse, so sensitivity to context is important. The same thing applies to the word 'dyke', though 'lesbian' has become a neutral term in academic discourse. Meanwhile the word 'homosexual' has itself become abusive, at least in spoken language, if pronounced with five unnaturally distinct syllables.

It can be harder still to judge the use of apparently discriminatory language by earlier writers. Wordsworth's poem *The Idiot Boy* was written at the end of the eighteenth century, a time when the word 'idiot' was used as a medical term to describe a person born with learning difficulties. This was also a period in which well-to-do families would often farm out such children in order to escape from the stigma associated with them, something which happened to Jane Austen's brother George (and was to happen in the early twentieth century to George V's youngest son John). The rustic mother whose love for 'her idiot boy' is repeatedly stressed in Wordsworth's poem needs to be seen in contrast to social attitudes of this kind. Given the fact that his mother is described as 'almost three-score', we can deduce that Johnny may in fact already be a young man, though one who remains a boy – a child as well as a son – in his mother's anxious eyes. It is because of her unceasing care that his adventure in the poem, as he rides off alone to fetch the doctor to attend their ailing neighbour old Susan Gale, is something unprecedented in his experience. Though he fails in his mission, he still succeeds in healing Susan, whose shared concern as Johnny fails to come home cures her faster than the doctor could have done. More crucially, the poem enables the reader to glimpse through Johnny's eyes what we ourselves would only be able to see if, in Blake's phrase, 'the doors of perception were cleansed'.[25] The boy who returns from riding alone through the mysterious night world has only the words of day to describe it with, and for this very reason his view of it is not obscured by the normalizing veil of habit. His eerie vision of night as day turned inside out transforms the prosy jog-trot of the verse into poetry of the kind which, for susceptible readers, makes the hairs stand up on the back of the neck.

> 'The cocks did crow to-whoo, to-whoo,
> 'And the sun did shine so cold.'
> – Thus answered Johnny in his glory.
> And that was all his travel's story.

While it is important not to misjudge Wordsworth's poem on account of its vocabulary, it is equally important, when discussing or writing about it, not to refer to its protagonist as 'the idiot'. The tutor who put *Lyrical Ballads* on the syllabus, or the examiner who marks your essay, or one or more of the fellow students who listen to your seminar presentation, may have a sibling or a child with learning difficulties.

Titles

This heading really encompasses two separate problems: how to choose a title for your essay and how to refer to the titles of books and their component parts. Let us begin with your choice of an essay title. The first point to make clear about titles is that every essay should have one. (It should also be clearly marked with its writer's name or examination number.) Your title can be the simplest one possible:

Milton's *Comus*

It can be a brief indication of the theme of your essay:

Patterns of Darkness and Light in Milton's *Comus*

It can take the form of an apt quotation – with an explanatory subtitle if necessary – from the author you are discussing, from a critic who seems to you either illuminatingly right or perversely wrong about your author, or from some other work which seems to you to be relevant:

'Complete Steel': Chastity in Milton's *Comus*

'Inelegantly splendid and tediously instructive':
the Deficiencies of Milton's Masque

Milton's 'Tulgy Wood': Moral Victory in *Comus*

It can even be an intriguing and mysterious phrase which leaves the subject matter of the essay unexplained, though in that case you will be well advised to enlighten the reader in your opening paragraph.

The two things to beware of are the title which sounds like an exam question:

Compare and contrast *L'Allegro* and *Il Penseroso*.

Paradise Lost is a flawed epic. Discuss.

and the title which you treat as an exam question by allowing it to trap you into writing a whole essay on a subject in which you lost interest after the second paragraph. If you find that new and unexpected ideas begin to develop as you write your essay, don't strangle the ideas because they conflict with your original title. Change the title. Better still, write the essay first and choose the title afterwards; it is your subject, not your title, that needs to be decided in advance.

The problem of referring to other people's titles is simply one of typography. Your readers have to be able to distinguish between Hamlet the Prince of Denmark and Hamlet the tragedy. You will make this easier for them by italicizing the latter: *Hamlet*. If you are forced to swap the keyboard for the biro (during a power-cut or a closed exam) you should underline titles instead, since underlining is the proof-reader's way of telling the typesetter that a word or phrase should be italicized: Dante's <u>Divina Commedia</u>. If you want to refer to a subsection of a larger work, you should use inverted commas:

Erich Auerbach's essay 'The Brown Stocking' in *Mimesis*

Individual poems count as whole works, and thus should have their titles italicized, unless you are referring to them in the context of a larger work (such as a collection of poems) of which they form a part:

George Herbert's poem *Easter-wings*

George Herbert's poem 'Easter-wings' in *The Temple*

Naming your author

The problem of how to refer to your author is covered by a simple rule (although with one or two exceptions): look at the title page. Whenever you use an author's whole name rather than his or her surname (except in footnotes or end-notes, of which more in Chapter 10), you should use the form under which the work was published: thus George (not G.) Eliot for the novelist, T. S. (not Thomas) Eliot for the poet and Dorothy L. (not just Dorothy) Sayers for the crime writer.

However, while George Eliot is still known by her pseudonym (and would be referred to as Mary Ann Evans only by a writer concerned with her life rather than her novels), Ellis Bell, for example, has long since had her cover blown, so you should ignore the title page of the first edition of *Wuthering Heights* and refer to its author as Emily Brontë. You should also ignore the now obsolete tradition which led to married Victorian women writers being published under their husbands' surnames (or even, as in the case of Mrs Humphry Ward, their husbands' full names) prefaced by a respectable Mrs. In these post-feminist days it is usual to refer to Elizabeth Gaskell, not Mrs Gaskell.

One exception to all the above is Dante Alighieri, who (to the relief of non-Italianists everywhere) is usually referred to simply by his forename.

If you want to refer to a writer that few people have ever heard of, then use the whole of his or her name the first time it occurs in your essay. Remember, too, that such a name will not speak for itself, so give some explanation of its significance: 'Jemima Sprockett, the little-known late-Victorian science-fiction writer . . .'

Making yourself clear

Mistakes in syntax, and obscurities of thought and expression generally, are often due to the essayist becoming so involved in a private struggle with the subject matter that the reader is forgotten. The student who exclaims, 'But *I* know what I meant!' is thinking of the essay as something wholly personal, like a diary, not as something communicated. You can cure yourself of this kind of solipsism by setting yourself the challenge of writing so that any intelligent lay person, including your granny, would be able to follow your argument. Sometimes, though, obscurity is due to the fact that the writer really doesn't know what he or she means but hopes that writing down a pastiche of the kind of prose generally found in essays will magically cause meaning to appear. If you have this problem, you need to get into the habit of working out what you are actually trying to say in each and every sentence before you write it down. Don't expect the sentence itself to do your thinking for you. Any sentence which, on serious consideration, turns out not to mean anything in particular is just padding and should be cut.

It is also possible to get into a syntactic tangle by writing needlessly long and complicated sentences in which the writer, as well as the reader, becomes hopelessly lost and confused. Over-long sentences are often the result of an honourable ambition to tackle ideas in all their complexity, so, if you have this problem, remember that simplifying your prose doesn't necessarily mean simplifying your ideas. An interesting and original thought will be more impressive if it is lucidly expressed, just as a silly or muddled one will not be improved by being wrapped in wet flannel. The American novelist Mark Twain, a believer in the efficacy of short sentences, gives a brilliant description of how the young writer (female as well as male) should compose the occasional long one:

> he will make sure that there are no folds in it, no vaguenesses, no parenthetical interruptions of its view as a whole; when he has done with it, it won't be a sea-serpent with half of its arches under water; it will be a torch-light procession.[26]

A striking illustration of the importance of clarity in conveying complex ideas is given by the materials scientist J. E. Gordon, writing about Young's Modulus, a fundamental concept in engineering which enables the elasticity of materials to be precisely measured, helping to prevent ships from sinking and buildings and bridges from falling down. Thomas Young, who published the first definition of the modulus in 1807, was a polymath and a genius. However:

> It was said of Young by one of his contemporaries that 'His words were not those in familiar use, and the arrangement of his ideas seldom the same as those he conversed with. He was therefore worse calculated than any man I ever knew for the communication of knowledge.'[27]

The truth of this is only too evident in his own definition of the modulus, which reads as follows:

> The modulus of the elasticity of any substance is a column of the same substance, capable of producing a pressure on its base which is to the weight causing a certain degree of compression as the length of the substance is to the diminution of its length.

Not surprisingly, the Admiralty responded, 'Though science is much respected by their Lordships and your paper is much esteemed, it is too learned . . . in short it is not understood'; and ships went on sinking and buildings and bridges went on falling down until the engagingly named French engineer Claude-Louis-Marie-Henri Navier found a better way of putting it in 1826:

$$E = stress / strain$$

To be fair to Young, Navier's equation depended on the work of yet another scientist, Augustin Cauchy, who, in 1822, was the first to define the all-important concepts of stress and strain; so the elegant lucidity of Navier's equation actually required the combined genius of no fewer than three brilliant minds.

Even if your prose has the inspired clarity of Navier's equation, it is still a good idea to check through your essay carefully before handing it in. If you do have difficulties with syntax, it helps to read the essay aloud, marking the sentences which sound wrong or funny, as a preliminary to making corrections.

Chapter 7

Some common bad advice

'Tell the examiners what they want to know'

This exhortation, sensible enough in itself, is generally taken to mean that there is a concrete body of information about the text under discussion (or, worse still, a series of 'points' about it) which the examiners will expect to receive from every candidate. The absurdity of this can be tested by taking any famous work of literature at random and skimming through the various critical accounts of it to be found on the shelves of even the most poorly stocked university library. Whichever text you happen to pick, you will find that the critics, far from being in accord, are as contradictory, and sometimes as contentious, as it is possible for them to be. There is no consensus, and no guarantee that any particular viewpoint is the one to trust. There are many and diverse ways of being right about a work of art.

It remains true, however, that there is something the examiners want you to tell them. They want to be told, as any reader of literary criticism wants to be told, something new and interesting and unexpected about the text, or failing that something familiar expressed in a way that makes it new. You are much more likely to give them this experience if you say what you really think about the text, rather than what you think they think you ought to think about it.

'Quote sparingly'

This advice is often given by teachers who believe that the purpose of teaching literature in schools is to get their students through public examinations. It is wholly pragmatic advice, and is based on the (probably erroneous) assumption that you will not be able to learn by heart more than three consecutive lines of anything. Since it follows from this that you will not be able to quote more than three consecutive lines of anything in a closed exam, you are urged never to do so under any circumstances. I have already dealt at some length with the problem of how to quote. It suffices to reiterate here that you should quote what will best serve to illustrate your point, neither more nor less. Sometimes a single phrase, or a single line of verse, will be enough. Sometimes you will need a whole paragraph or a whole sonnet.

'Never say I'

I do not know the reason for this odd advice. It may spring from an exaggerated respect for humility, a feeling that it would be arrogant of the essay-writer even to acknowledge that he or she exists. On the other hand, it may be an attempt to bolster up the essay-writer's views, since to follow such advice leaves you with the options either of imitating the detachment of a scientific paper by writing entirely in the passive voice – 'Dickens's emotional appeal to the individual reader will be discussed in this essay' – or of making a lordly choice between those grand pronouns 'one' and 'we'. It is dangerous advice to follow, not only because of the risk of sounding pompous and impersonal but also because you will be prevented from making the distinction between what you personally feel and what most readers are likely to feel.

For an illustration of the peculiar force which an acknowledgement of personal feeling can give to an otherwise dispassionate account, try the effect of deleting the first seven words from Dr Johnson's famous note on Shakespeare's *All's Well That Ends Well*.

> I cannot reconcile my heart to Bertram; a man noble without generosity and young without truth; who marries Helen as a coward and leaves her as a profligate: when she is dead by his unkindness, sneaks home to a second marriage, is accused by a woman whom he has wronged, defends himself by falsehood, and is dismissed to happiness.[1]

'An essay should have a beginning, a middle and an end'

This seems on the face of it to be a harmless if unnecessary statement, since an essay, like any other piece of writing, will inevitably have a beginning and an end, and what comes between a beginning and an end must obviously be a middle. In fact it is a statement loaded with misleading implications. To start with, there is something odd, on closer inspection, about the idea of an essay having a middle. A poem (like a play or a novel) will have a beginning and an end and these will often be particularly vivid and memorable, but we never think of a poem as having a middle. What we think of in contrast to the beginning and end of the poem is the poem itself, the whole poem seen as an entity. To say of an essay that it must have a beginning, a middle and an end is to say, in effect, that the middle is the real essay but that this naked middle must be made decent and acceptable by being dressed up in an Introduction and a Conclusion.

There are occasions – when your essay is going to say something very contentious or attempt to prove something long disputed – when it is useful to begin by stating what you intend to do and end by underlining the fact that you have done it. For obvious reasons, this is standard practice in the writing of scientific papers. All too often, though, the idea that an essay on literature must have an Introduction and a Conclusion leads the writer to sandwich the meat of the argument between two bits of low-fibre, pre-sliced prose. All tutors and examiners are familiar with the essay which begins, in effect, 'All the poets of the seventeenth century said, "Rhubarb, rhubarb, rhubarb," and in this Marvell was no exception', and which ends, 'Thus we see that Marvell was outstanding among the poets of the seventeenth century for the clarity and vigour with which he said, "Rhubarb, rhubarb, rhubarb".' What comes in between may be an acute and subtle analysis of Marvell's poetry, but the essay will still leave a stale taste in the reader's mouth, and with good reason. Your opening sentences create the expectations, whether of enjoyment or of boredom, with which the reader approaches the rest of your essay. Your closing sentences, simply by their position, are the ones which remain most vividly in the reader's mind after the essay has been put down. If you remember this, and write with a sense that the argument of your essay stretches from its first sentence to its last, then your prose is much more likely to remain alive and interesting throughout.

Chapter 8

Spelling, punctuation and grammar

Spelling

> This recommendation of steadiness and uniformity does not pro-
> ceed from an opinion, that particular combinations of letters have
> much influence on human happiness; or that truth may not be
> successfully taught by modes of spelling fanciful and erroneous:
> I am not yet so lost in lexicography, as to forget that *words are the*
> *daughters of earth, and that things are the sons of heaven*. Language is
> only the instrument of science, and words are but the signs of
> ideas: I wish, however, that the instrument might be less apt to
> decay, and that signs might be permanent, like the things which
> they denote.
>
> Samuel Johnson, *Preface to The English Dictionary* (1755)

Correct spelling is generally thought of as the hallmark of literacy,
and yet not only have many great writers, including Keats and Jane
Austen, been poor spellers but some of the greatest, including Shakespeare, did not possess the concept of standardized spelling at all. As
Samuel Johnson admits in the *Preface* to his great *Dictionary of the*
English Language, sticking to 'particular combinations of letters' is not
an essential component of effective writing. This will seem less
surprising if we remember that spelling is simply a system of conventions for indicating (rather than actually reproducing) the sounds of
speech and is not something inherent in the nature or meanings
of words. There was no practical need for 'correct', as opposed to
phonetically comprehensible, spelling until people began to arrange
words and names in alphabetical order. The thirty-four versions of
the name Shakespeare used by the poet's family ranged from Chacsper
to Shaxspere, taking in such variants as Shackspire, Shagspere and

Shakysper along the way.[1] This doesn't tell us that the entire Shakespeare clan was dyslexic but simply that the phone-book and the library catalogue had yet to be invented. In fact, the first English dictionary, Robert Cawdrey's *A Table Alphabeticall of Hard Usual English Words*, was not published until 1604, when Shakespeare himself was forty years old, and even that, despite its title, was not arranged in strictly alphabetical order.

There were, in fact, some sensible reasons why the scribes and printers of the past chose not to adopt a single mandatory spelling for each word in the English language. Before the Norman conquest, monastic scribes did adhere to quite strict spelling conventions, but their work was mainly intended for a local readership and reflected local pronunciation. English spelling began to be standardized at the end of the fifteenth century with the introduction of printing, although unfortunately this had the effect of fixing the written form of the language at a time when it was undergoing the major changes known as the great vowel shift. Elizabethan scholars further complicated matters by introducing new etymological spellings to reflect what they took to be the Greek or Latin derivations of words, many of which had in fact come into English via Old French. During this period, printers deliberately made use of variant spellings in order to justify their pages (give them a fairly uniform right-hand margin).

The gradual move towards standardization was not complete even with the publication of Samuel Johnson's *Dictionary of the English Language* in the mid eighteenth century, influential though that was. Johnson's *Dictionary*, the first English dictionary in the modern sense, contained only 43,000 words (roughly a tenth of the number in the first edition of *The Oxford English Dictionary*), and since, despite his desire for uniformity, Johnson was aware that the task of the lexicographer is essentially descriptive rather than prescriptive, he included variant spellings of some words. What is more, as G. H. Vallins shows in his classic book on the subject,[2] even approximately standardized spelling was for a long time regarded as a printer's skill and the private letter-writer and diarist was still free to spell by ear. Queen Elizabeth I, though a highly educated woman fluent in five languages, spelt with rough robustness, but the little boy who in 1730 boasted to his father, 'This Letter is of my one spilling'[3] was already beginning to feel that orthodoxy matters, and nowadays the educated writer is expected to stick to conventional spelling at all times. However, spelling has not been completely standardized even today, since not only are there a number of words the variants of which are regarded as equally correct[4] but British and American English have different but mutually intelligible conventions.[5]

Despite all this, it is important to spell correctly simply to prevent your readers from thinking you ignorant, but it is not always easy to do so. Spelling is an unstable skill (teachers tend to pick up the mis-spellings of their students) and it depends far more on shape recognition and visual memory than on an ear for, and a knowledge of, language. If your visual memory is poor, you will find spelling a struggle. In addition, the invention firstly of email, with its culture of light-hearted disregard for conventions, and then of texting, which effectively returns the user to the pre-vowel alphabet of ancient Hebrew, means that orthodox spelling has gone back to being a printer's convention – though now the printer is the one linked to the computer on which you write your essays. It is even harder to master a set of often irrational conventions if you largely ignore them during much of your everyday life.

There are several sensible measures you can take to improve your spelling. The first is to keep a dictionary on your desk and make a habit of checking every word about which you feel at all uncertain; the second is to pin up a list of the words you most commonly get wrong; and the third, and most important, is to learn to use a spell check. Learn is the operative word here. Despite what old–fashioned school teachers may have told you, computer spell checks don't enable you to cheat by effortlessly doing your spelling for you. A spell check is a kind of sorcerer's apprentice which will create havoc if you uncritically accept all its suggestions, especially if your essay includes quotations from Middle English. To use a spell check successfully, you will need to remember the following points:

1: Always use a spell check with a dictionary. Accepting substitute words you aren't sure of from a spell check is as dangerous as taking candy from a stranger.

2: Computer spell checks come with a limited, and often specialized, vocabulary. If they fail to recognize a word, that doesn't necessarily mean that it is wrongly spelt. You should take the trouble to customize your spell check to your own usage, prose style and subject matter.

3: Your computer spell check will only recognize proper names if you add them to its vocabulary (and if you type them in wrong it will recognize them wrong). It certainly won't tell you how to spell either Odysseus or Ulysses.

4: Not all spell checks offer you the choice between British and American spelling.

5: No spell check can deal with homophones (words which sound the same but are spelt differently) so you will have to find another way of remembering the difference between 'principal' and 'principle'.

6: Spell checks can't pick up typos if they take the form of other existing words; they won't turn 'soda' back into 'sofa'.

7: On the plus side, your spell check can help to improve your own spelling if you use it to check individual words you are unsure of and try to memorize what it tells you.

One oddity of the British obsession with spelling is that it doesn't extend to the accents in foreign words, despite the fact that these really are essential components, not dispensable frills. An accent tells you how a word should be pronounced (as in the French *écrire*), or where the stress falls in it (as in the Italian *città*), or even (as in the case of Swedish ö or Danish ø) that the letter in question is an addition to the Roman alphabet. Don't leave them out.

Students of literature not only need to be able to spell competently themselves, they also occasionally need to consult facsimiles or scholarly editions which reproduce the orthography of earlier historical periods. This means that you need to be able to make sense of spelling which differs from present-day conventions:

Cover her face: Mine eyes dazell: she di'd yong.[6]

and also to recognize that what looks like an *f* without a cross stroke is a 'long *s*' (a form of the letter which continued to be used until the eighteenth century) and that what looks like a *y* may actually be a 'thorn', an Old English consonant which was derived from runic script and was pronounced *th* (so Ye Olde Teashoppe is actually pronounced The Old Teashop, although the thorn only survived until the fifteenth century, and the English didn't become tea drinkers until the eighteenth).

Paradoxically, reading this kind of text can sometimes be easier for people who have problems with their own spelling than it is for those who have an overly rigid attachment to orthodoxy – which leads us neatly to the subject of the next section.

Dealing with dyslexia

Dyslexia is a very common specific learning difficulty which can cause a range of problems associated with language processing and short-term memory. In addition to problems with spelling (which may be particularly marked with proper names, foreign languages and unfamiliar forms of language such as Middle English), these may include difficulties with punctuation and lay-out, difficulties in proof-reading and using a spell check, and problems with structuring essays and organizing material. Students with dyslexia may also experience difficulty with taking and reading back research notes owing to slow and untidy handwriting, and with writing up essays owing to slow and inaccurate typing. Dyslexia has a known genetic component so it tends to run in families, and may be associated with allergic disorders such as hay fever and asthma, and also with left-handedness.

If you know that you are, or suspect that you may be, dyslexic, it is important to keep the problem in perspective. To start with, there is no connection between dyslexia, mild or severe, and low IQ. Indeed, many highly creative and successful people have been, and are, dyslexic, including the novelist Gustave Flaubert and the poet W. B. Yeats (not to mention Albert Einstein and Pablo Picasso). Dyslexia is a disability on a par with poor eyesight or hearing, though unfortunately it can't be corrected by some linguistic equivalent of spectacles or a hearing aid. Instead, people with dyslexia have to develop compensatory strategies to get around the problem, often leading to an increased capacity for lateral thinking, which may help to account for the known connection between dyslexia and high achievement in mathematics and the sciences.

Nor is the popular description of dyslexia as 'word-blindness' an accurate one. Indeed, surprisingly enough, dyslexia can actually lead to greater skill with words in some important respects. Margaret J. Snowling describes, in her authoritative book on dyslexia, the results of a study she carried out in 1983 with Professor Uta Frith in which dyslexic children, who had difficulty reading 'nonwords' (words with no meaning used to test phonetic skills) proved to be '*better* than their reading-age matched controls' at reading 'sentences containing homographs such as "they started to *row* across the river" or "she waved her wand and the boat became *minute*".[7] The dyslexic children had learnt to compensate for their phonetic difficulties by becoming more attentive to context than the children in the control group who had no problem with the nonwords. Snowling also makes the point that 'dyslexic children who read a lot quite obviously have more chance of developing a sight vocabulary than children who shy away from literary activities'.[8] University students with dyslexia are all, by definition, people who have developed high-level compensatory strategies. When the increased ability to think laterally which went into developing those skills is combined with patience and determination, such students often end up outstripping their peers.

If you know that you are dyslexic, it is sensible to make sure that your university department is aware of it and has a copy of any assessment documentation. You may need extra time in closed exams, and you will certainly need examiners to be aware that they should disregard spelling mistakes and minor glitches in punctuation and layout. It is also sensible to take advantage of any study skills sessions on offer to dyslexic students. If you suspect that you may be dyslexic, you need to find out if your university's disability services include dyslexia assessment.

However, beating dyslexia is mainly a question of adopting a professional attitude to your work, identifying your specific problems and working out how to minimize them by increased care in those particular areas. For instance, if you have problems with structuring an argument, you need to develop an efficient way of making a detailed preliminary essay plan. If you have difficulty with spelling, you not only need to learn how to use a computer spell check, you also need strategies for dealing with those things that spell checks won't automatically help you with. Here are a few suggestions:

1: If you have a problem with proper names, you can customize your spell check before you start writing your essay on Yeats to ensure it doesn't turn into an essay on Yates. Check carefully that you have done the customizing the right way round.

2: In the case of homophones (words which sound the same but are spelt differently, such as 'there' and 'their') and near homophones (such as 'quite' and 'quiet') spell checks are no help at all. Try pinning up a list of paired explanatory phrases (again, double checking that you haven't got them the wrong way round):

All *quiet* on the western front.
You are *quite* right.

3: It is important to remember that spell checks work only if they know where the words begin and end, so remember that you need to leave a space after full stops, commas and other punctuation marks. Dashes need a space both before and after, while hyphens should have neither.

4: Since spelling is a visual skill, it often helps to scribble down the possible variants of a word and look at them. You may find when you do this that you can spot which one is correct.

5: A good old-fashioned dictionary has the advantage over a spell check of giving you definitions of the words that you are doubtful about. Make sure you buy a hardbacked one, and get yourself into the habit of using it. By the time the spine falls off, you may well be expert enough to correct other people's spelling mistakes. (I speak from experience here.)

Finally, it is important to remember that there is only one thing which can hold you back, and that is lack of confidence. If you are someone who was scolded for carelessness or laziness at school when you were actually doing more than your best, or conversely if your parents or grandparents treated your dyslexia as a major handicap in life, it can be quite hard to get rid of the resultant sense of anxiety and low self-esteem. However, the very fact that you are now a university student of literature proves that, far from being someone with poor verbal skills, you are actually someone with serious verbal talents, as well as the added maturity which comes from having had to struggle to maximize those talents. Be proud of yourself. The sky is your limit.

Punctuation and syntax

SYNTAX is a word, which comes from the Greek. It means, in that language, the *joining of several things together*; and, as used by grammarians, it means those principles and rules, which teach us how to put words together so as to form *sentences*. It means, in short, *sentence-making . . . Syntax* will teach you how to give all your words their *proper* situations, or places, when you come to put them together into sentences. And here you will have to do with *points* as well as with words. The *points* are four in number, the *Comma*, the *Semi-Colon*, the *Colon*, and the *Period*. Besides these Points, there are certain *marks*, such as the *mark of interrogation*, for instance; and, to use these points and marks properly is, as you will by-and-by find, a matter of very great importance.

William Cobbett, *Grammar of the English Language* (1823)

Punctuation, William Cobbett's system of 'points' and 'marks', is in fact a more important feature of written language than standard-ized spelling, and yet, paradoxically, it is possible to dispense with it altogether. Stranger still, far from simply noting the pauses in spoken language, it actually departs further from them than modern English spelling does from the phonetic transcription of the sounds made by native speakers. We are all given the idea in primary school that punctuation was invented to prevent readers aloud from running out of breath, a point of view shared by the playwright and poet Ben Jonson in his *English Grammar* (first published in 1640, three years after its author's death). Unlike Cobbett, he tackled the subject of what he called 'the distinction of sentences' at the very end of his book.

> All the parts of *Syntaxe* have already been declared. There resteth one generall Affection of the whole, dispersed thorow every member thereof, as the bloud is thorow the body; and consisteth in the breathing, when we pronounce any *Sentence*; For, whereas our breath is by nature so short, that we cannot continue without a stay to speake long together; it was thought necessarie, as well for the speakers ease, as for the plainer deliverance of the things spoken, to invent this meanes, whereby men pausing a pretty while, the whole speech might never the worse be understood.[9]

Jonson, of course, lived before any means had been invented for recording speech apart from writing it down, and he was also a professional dramatist working in a theatre where the acting style involved declaiming highly formalized dialogue, often in blank verse, which may well have seemed far more naturalistic at the time than it does to us today. In fact, if you analyse passages of recorded speech, you find that, even in the case of highly educated speakers, both the syntax and the 'punctuation' are quite unlike what we find in writ-ten language. Not only is it almost impossible to divide up normal speech into conventional sentences, the system of pauses has as much to do with musical phrasing, combined with moments of reflection while searching for the next word, as it has to do with the highlighting of syntax. Here is a short extract from an oral history interview with a retired doctor. Apart from the interviewer's questions, signalled by intonation, I have marked all the pauses with vertical lines. Incidentally, the interviewee's final 'and' does not signal that something more is about to be added, as it would in a piece of written text, but is a way of breaking off the subject.

now this was during the war | when soldiers came to York | and they obviously got married | 1941 at the beginning of the war | they obviously got married | in a hurry | I remember that man | I remember his wife too |

what do you remember about them? what were they like?

just that they were a very happy couple | and that | they went to Liverpool as far as I know | and | they came to our house actually | and | they were a very happy couple I remember | they | sort of spread out into the family because they were | so overjoyed at being married and |[10]

The famous Renaissance Venetian printer and publisher Aldus Manutius put his finger on the real purpose of punctuation in 1466, while also making the important point that this is a subject on which educated people can hold opposing views. Indeed, unlike modern spelling, many aspects of punctuation are still subject to individual taste even today.

That learned men are well known to disagree on this subject of punctuation is in itself a proof, that the knowledge of it, in theory and practise, is of some importance. I myself have learned by experience, that, if ideas that are difficult to understand are properly separated, they become clearer; and that, on the other hand, through defective punctuation, many passages are confused and distorted to such a degree, that sometimes they can with difficulty be understood, or even cannot be understood at all.[11]

William Cobbett, for whom clarity is the most important feature of any piece of writing, is so aware of the role of punctuation in preventing ambiguity or misunderstanding that he deals with it at the

very start of his consideration of syntax, punching home the point
that more than grammar is at stake in true radical style with a
politically charged anecdote:

> A memorable proof of the great importance of attending to
> *points* was given to the English nation in the year 1817. A
> Committee of the House of Lords made a report to the House,
> respecting certain political clubs. A secretary of one of those
> clubs presented a petition to the House, in which he declared
> positively, and offered to prove at the bar, that a part of the
> report was *totally false*. At first their Lordships blustered: their
> high blood seemed to boil: but at last, the Chairman of the
> Committee apologized for the report by saying, that there ought
> to have been *a full point* where there was only a *comma*! and that
> it was this, which made that false, which would otherwise have
> been, and which was intended to be, true![12]

The moral of Cobbett's story is that punctuation is not just a
matter of learning a set of rules and applying them for the sake of
copybook correctness; it is a vital part of syntax and can be crucial in
making your meaning clear. Effective punctuation involves knowing
precisely what it is that you are trying to say and then thinking
intelligently about the shape and the logic of your sentences. The set
of rules, some of which are rules of thumb, comes into play to
enable you to make that shape and logic crystal clear to your reader.
We will come to the rules themselves later in the chapter, but first I
want to look briefly at another aspect of the subject which particularly affects students of English and foreign literature. Not only do
different historical periods or languages adopt different conventions
(such as the angle brackets which are used as speech-marks in Italian, or
the inverted question marks and exclamation marks which precede
interrogative or exclamative sentences in Spanish) but the punctuation
in works of literature can be very different from punctuation in
scholarly prose. Indeed sometimes it can be conspicuous by its absence.
  One of the most famous examples of this is Molly Bloom's
soliloquy at the end of James Joyce's *Ulysses*, a *tour de force* attempt by
a male novelist to imitate what the French feminist writer Hélène
Cixous was later to call *écriture féminine* (writing which employs a
'feminine' voice, and is thus able to explore meanings which lie beyond
the 'masculine' constraints of logic). Molly is not really soliloquizing
in the theatrical sense – she is thinking, not thinking aloud – but her

interminable sentence, unpunctuated except for the final full stop, is in fact a spirited monologue about her own life experience which the reader would have no difficulty at all in understanding if Joyce had punctuated it as speech. In fact, the whole thing is a conjuring trick; it is the mere absence of Cobbett's 'points' and 'marks' which makes us imagine that we are eavesdropping on Molly's thoughts. If we were to put the commas and full stops back, we would discover that, unlike much else in the novel, this isn't really 'difficult' writing at all. We would also, of course, be removing the veil of mock-obscurity which teasingly conceals from all but Joyce's most assiduous readers just how earthy many of Molly's reflections are.

If we turn from the fictive Molly (who, brilliantly as her voice is achieved, could be seen as simply a ventriloquist's doll) to a genuine example of *écriture feminine*, we will discover a more daring and creative abandonment of convention. The nineteenth-century American poet Emily Dickinson famously punctuated her poems almost entirely with dashes. Ernest Gowers, in *The Complete Plain Words*, says disparagingly:

> The dash is seductive; it tempts the writer to use it as a punctuation-maid-of-all-work that saves him the trouble of choosing the right stop. We all know letter-writers who carry this habit to the length of relying on one punctuation mark only – a nondescript symbol that might be a dash or might be something else.

For Emily Dickinson, the dash was a subtle musical device through which she could notate an emotional logic quite different from the syntactical one which Cobbett enjoined on the readers of his *English Grammar*. It is an important factor here that the bulk of Dickinson's enormous oeuvre remained unknown and unpublished during her lifetime, while in the few examples which did appear in print her punctuation had been normalized. Perhaps, though, it would be more accurate to say that it was her unwillingness to allow her work to be normalized (and not only in regard to its punctuation) which caused it to remain unpublished. She wrote to the essayist Thomas Wentworth Higginson (who has gone down in literary history as the critic who initially judged her verse too odd and delicate for publication and then edited out its idiosyncrasies after her death):

> I smile when you suggest that I delay 'to publish' – that being foreign to my thought, as Firmament to Fin –

If fame belonged to me, I could not escape her – if she did
not, the longest day would pass me on the chase – and the
approbation of my Dog, would forsake me – then – My
Barefoot-Rank is better –
    You think my gait 'spasmodic' – I am in danger – Sir –
    You think me 'uncontrolled' – I have no Tribunal.[13]

That small sample of her prose is sufficient to show that the
punctuation of her poems was not simply a literary device, and that
her independence of mind was allied to an extraordinarily keen ear
for precisely those nuances of spoken language which conventional
punctuation is not designed to capture. This will become clearer if
we look at one of the greatest of her poems. Notice, in particular,
how she slows down the tempo in the second stanza to convey the
evanescence of human life when viewed from the perspective of
astronomical time.

> Safe in their Alabaster Chambers –
> Untouched by Morning –
> And untouched by Noon –
> Lie the meek members of the Resurrection –
> Rafter of Satin – and Roof of Stone!
>
> Grand go the Years – in the Crescent – above them –
> Worlds scoop their Arcs –
> And Firmaments – row –
> Diadems – drop – and Doges – surrender –
> Soundless as dots – on a Disc of Snow –

Another nineteenth-century poet, John Clare, also largely dis-
pensed with punctuation, relying instead on the sheer lucidity of his
writing to make his meaning clear. Clare was a self-taught working man who was patronizingly celebrated by the literati as 'the
Northamptonshire peasant' and later neglected and forgotten by them.
(Similarly, even waiting for publication and fame until after her
death did not save Emily Dickinson from being labelled 'the Amherst
poetess'.) Unsurprisingly, given that his first book of poems was
published in 1820, Clare was unable to prevent his publisher from
'correcting' his poems. Here, to illustrate the way in which he
successfully pushed to the limits Ernest Gowers' excellent maxim
that 'meaning should wherever possible be clear without stops', are a

couple of extracts from his letters. In the first he turns a critical eye
on the kind of inscription which doubtless adorned the headstones
of the New England graves transfigured in Dickinson's poem, while in
the second, written in Northampton General Asylum where he spent
the last twenty-three years of his life, he looks back on the pleasures
of his childhood and youth.

> I should like to see good Epitaphs introduced into churches &
> churchyards in lieu of bad ones but there is a secret charm attached
> to the bad rhymes & worse metre of Stonecutters verses which
> will ever make them favourites of the lower orders & leave them
> not entirely discarded by the higher ones from whom the example
> should first come & that charm is that they are so full of flattery
> to the dead & we may walk into fifty churchyards & be universally
> told on every stone that its possessor died a good person & scarcely
> see it hinted in one that the living are not so good but they may
> improve thus will bad verses with neither moral or merit to
> entertain or improve the mind be opposed to the use of good
> ones that might be made to contain both
> (letter to Mrs Marianne Marsh, 19 October 1829)

> in my boyhood Solitude was the most talkative vision I met
> with Birds bees trees flowers all talked to me incessantly louder
> than the busy hum of men & who so wise as nature out of doors
> on the green grass by woods & streams under the beautiful
> sunny sky daily communing with God & not a word spoken
> (letter to his son Charles, February 1848)

Even if your prose is as lucid as Clare's, you can't afford to hand
in your essays without any punctuation at all – though his example
does serve as a useful reminder that if you have to punctuate in an
over-ingenious way to prevent misunderstanding or ambiguity then
it is probably better to recast your sentence. So here, to help you to
punctuate intelligently, is an explanation of the use of Cobbett's
points and marks, starting with the ones we use to end a sentence
(full stop, question mark, exclamation mark); followed by the stronger
pauses inside a sentence (colon, semicolon); then the most prob-
lematic of all punctuation marks, the comma; then apostrophes
and inverted commas; dashes and hyphens; brackets and ellipses; and
finally that other essential aid to making the structure of your argument clear: paragraphing.

Full stop

As everyone knows, a full stop is used to end a sentence, but it is not nearly so easy to define what a sentence is. While modern linguists such as Sidney Greenbaum take many pages attempting to do so,[14] William Cobbett, in his *Grammar of the English Language*, opts for the simplest possible solution to the problem: 'here I will just add that a *sentence*, used as a term in grammar, means one of those portions of words which are divided from the rest by a *single dot*, which is called a *period*, or full point'.[15] Unfortunately, it is not really the case that you can turn any sequence of words into a sentence by putting a full stop at the end. Going for a fairly simple solution myself, let me say that a sentence, at any rate for the purposes of academic essay-writing, needs to contain at least one main clause with a finite verb. A finite verb is one which is limited by number and person (unlike an infinitive or a participle). In English, finite verbs occur only in the present and past tense:

> The cat **sits** on the mat.
> The cat **sat** on the mat.

while other tenses are formed by combining finite auxiliary verbs with participles or infinitives or both:

> The cat **was** *sitting* on the mat.
> The cat **will** *sit* on the mat.
> The cat **will** *be sitting* on the mat.

If this seems rather technical and off-putting, you simply need to remember that all of the above examples are sentences, while the phrase 'the cat sitting on the mat' is not. Once you feel that difference, even if you would find it hard to define, you are unlikely to go wrong. (If, on the contrary, you are interested and would like to go into the subject in more detail, then you should consult Greenbaum's excellent *An Introduction to English Grammar*.)

A sentence which contains only one such clause is a *simple sentence*:

> James wanted to go to the Lighthouse.

If it contains two or more such clauses, usually linked by a co-ordinating conjunction (*and*, *but*, *or*) then it is a *compound sentence*:

James wanted to go to the Lighthouse, *but* his father said it would rain.

If it has a main clause and one or more subordinate clauses then it is a *complex sentence*:

> *Being too young to understand the risks of sailing in bad weather,* James wanted to go to the Lighthouse, *even though his father said it would rain.*

It is a common mistake, when writing complex sentences, to treat the subordinate clauses as if they were free-standing sentences, as in the following example from a student essay:

> Mr Ramsay's repeated murmuring of Cowper's line, 'we perished, each alone,' brings together two of the most troubling concepts for humankind. That of mortality and that of the inherently solitary nature of the individual. Two boundaries of the human condition which the characters in *To the Lighthouse* constantly strive to transcend, but cannot.

The second and third 'sentences' here are actually leaning against the first one for support, as will become apparent if we pull the prop away and make them try to stand up on their own.

> That of mortality and that of the inherently solitary nature of the individual.

Since this does not contain a verb of any kind, it is not even a subordinate clause but simply a phrase, while the third 'sentence', though it does have a finite verb ('strive') clearly require a main clause, however brief, to make it grammatically complete:

> *There are* two boundaries of the human condition which the characters . . . constantly strive to transcend, but cannot.

In fact the whole passage is really a single complex sentence, as will become clear if we alter the punctuation. (Incidentally, the way in which I have chosen to do so is only one out of several possibilities.)

> Mr Ramsay's repeated murmuring of Cowper's line, 'we perished, each alone,' brings together two of the most troubling

concepts for humankind, that of mortality and that of the inherently solitary nature of the individual – two boundaries of the human condition which the characters in *To the Lighthouse* constantly strive to transcend but cannot.

As well as being used at the ends of sentences, full stops can also be used after initials and abbreviations (such as p. for page, ed. for edited and trans. for translated). Nowadays this usage is optional, but if you want to omit the full stops, on the grounds that they are fussy and redundant, you may need to customize your spell check accordingly; and if you eventually move on to writing academic books or journal articles, you will find that this, along with much else, is covered by publishers' style guides, which tend to err on the side of formality.

Question mark

Question marks are used only after direct questions, while indirect ones are followed by a full stop:

'Why can't we go the Lighthouse?' asked James.

James asked why they couldn't go to the Lighthouse.

Except in the case of questions within quotations or passages of reported speech (as in the first of the two examples above), you should use a question mark only at the end of a sentence, even if that sentence contains more than one question:

Why is Mr Ramsay so eager to thwart his son's desire to go to the Lighthouse, and why does Mrs Ramsay continue to feed James's hopes?

Exclamation mark

In informal writing, exclamation marks are often used whenever the writer wants to draw attention to something, with particularly significant points being signalled by multiple exclamation marks and absurd or otherwise striking details by exclamation marks in brackets. In formal prose, however, exclamation marks are correct only at the end of exclamations, so you shouldn't use them to draw attention to the daring of your author and your own broad-mindedness in alluding to it, as in the following rather touching example from a student essay on *Ulysses*:

> The day is hot and sticky, and Bloom dreams of himself in the bath with his penis floating languidly!

Since exclamations (sentences such as 'Help!', 'Drop the gun!' and 'God save the Queen!') are rare in academic prose, you are likely to need to use exclamation marks only in quotations. However, you do need to be aware that, like question marks, they can be used only at the end of a sentence.

Colon

A colon is not a kind of double-decker full stop, so should not be followed by a capital letter. It is used to indicate that what follows it is a clarification or elaboration of what precedes it, whether that clarification consists of a word, a phrase, or something longer and more complicated:

> Mr Ramsay wanted only one thing: attention.

> James wanted only one thing: to go to the Lighthouse.

> Mrs Ramsay was torn between several competing urges: to comfort her son; to mollify her husband; and to have some time to herself in which to complete the stocking she was knitting for the Lighthouse keeper's little boy.

Colons can also be used to usher in a quotation or example, and to separate the main title of a book or essay from its subtitle:

> Finishing the Brown Stocking:
> Altruism and Desire in *To the Lighthouse*

Semicolon

The semicolon can be used instead of a conjunction to join two or more sentences into one:

> Mrs Ramsay indulged her children; Mr Ramsay felt that they could not learn too early that 'life is difficult'.

Note that a comma is not a strong enough stop to be used in this way. Semicolons are also used to separate items in a list if those items are phrases or clauses rather than single words:

> Mrs Ramsay intended to pack a pile of old magazines; an un-wanted book or two; several ounces of pipe tobacco; and the pair of reddish-brown stockings she had knitted for the Light-house keeper's little boy.

Comma

G. V. Carey, in his classic little book on punctuation, *Mind the Stop*, calls the comma 'the most ubiquitous, elusive and discretionary of all stops'.[16] Commas have a multitude of uses, and can cause havoc with your sentence if you misuse them, but they are also often optional, though you need to make sure that, when you do use them, it is in the right places. It is probably simplest to list the various uses, of which the most important are:

1: *To join two sentences into one*: A comma is used after a conjunction to join two sentences into one, though if the conjunction is 'and' the comma is optional, since the 'and' itself joins the two parts of the sentence together.

> Mr Ramsay has an unyielding approach to life and James is just as stubborn.

> James is determined not to forgive his father, but Cam is far less resolute.

2: *To bracket off parts of a sentence*: Commas can be used rather like the brackets in an algebraic equation to make the structure of a sentence clear to the reader. Any phrase or clause enclosed in a pair of bracketing commas must be one which could be lifted out of the sentence without disrupting its syntax. Pairs of bracketing commas can often be omitted, but if you leave out just one of a pair then confusion results. (The only exception to this is where the bracketed phrase comes right at the beginning or end of a sentence, in which case the full stop either of the previous sentence or of the sentence itself acts as the other comma in the pair.) If we take some examples of sentences where the bracketing has gone wrong and repunctuate them, it will become clear how this works.

> The answer, I believe is to do with the place the novel has claimed, in the history of modernism.

Here the first comma is the orphaned half of a bracketing pair, while the second comma is a desperate attempt to make the first comma bracket *something*. If we lift out the bracketed section, the sentence reads:

> The answer in the history of modernism.

We can rescue the sentence, and highlight its structure, by putting that second comma back where it belongs:

> The answer, I believe, is to do with the place the novel has claimed in the history of modernism.

In the next example, the omission of the second of a pair of bracketing commas has dramatically altered the meaning of the sentence:

> Thus it can be seen that Gerontion, in denying Christ cannot find interior order, and as a result is left to face his approaching end in a state of utter spiritual aridity.

Gerontion is not really 'denying Christ cannot find interior order' as will become clear if we restore the missing comma:

> Thus it can be seen that Gerontion, in denying Christ, cannot find interior order, and as a result is left to face his approaching end in a state of utter spiritual aridity.

In the third example, an unnecessary comma is committing the solecism of dividing a subject from its verb:

> Virginia Woolf, uses the device of the stream of consciousness to explore the inner lives of her characters.

If we give this redundant comma a companion plus a phrase to bracket, the problem disappears, because a bracketed phrase can in theory be lifted out of the sentence, complete with its flanking commas, restoring the connection between Virginia Woolf and her verb:

Virginia Woolf, in *To the Lighthouse*, uses the device of the stream of consciousness to explore the inner lives of her characters.

3: *To link a series of adjectives or the items in a list*: It is a matter of taste whether the 'and' which ushers in the final item in the list should be prefaced by a comma. This is known as the Oxford comma and is part of the house style of Oxford University Press. The counter argument is that 'and' is a joining word, so already does the job of a comma. People can get very heated about this, but it doesn't really matter which convention you choose to adopt, provided you remember never to insert a comma between the final adjective of a series and the subject it qualifies. However, there are two tricky cases which need to be considered separately. The first is where one of the items in a list takes the form of '*x* and *y*': in this case you definitely need the Oxford comma to avoid confusion about what goes with what:

Cinderella, Red Riding Hood, Hansel and Gretel, and Rapunzel

The second is where the final adjective in a series is actually part of the subject which the other adjectives are qualifying. The rule about not inserting a comma between the final adjective in a series and the subject it qualifies means that you have to write 'innocent, trusting Red Riding Hood', not 'innocent, trusting, Red Riding Hood'.

Commas are also used:

4: *When someone is being addressed by their proper name or title*: This is called the vocative comma. If Juliet, instead of wishing Romeo had a different name, had been wondering where he had got to, Shakespeare would have written not 'wherefore art thou Romeo?' but 'where art thou, Romeo?'

5: *To introduce direct speech*: This can best be explained by a couple of examples:

Juliet exclaims, 'O Romeo, Romeo! wherefore art thou Romeo?' Romeo murmurs to himself, 'Shall I hear more, or shall I speak at this?'[17]

6: *With commenting but not with defining relative clauses*: Relative clauses are ones beginning with 'who' or 'which'. Whether you write 'the man who . . .' or 'the man, who . . .' depends on whether the relative clause is one which *defines* who or what the man in question actually is or merely one which *comments* on him. The following two examples should make this clear:

> 'I am the Cat who walks by himself, and all places are alike to me.'[18]

> He is holding up his hand to call the Dog, who has swum across to the other side of the river, looking for rabbits.[19]

7: *To stand in for words which have been omitted rather than repeated*: An example will be sufficient to explain this. In Alexander Pope's line, 'To err is human; to forgive, divine', the comma stands in for a repetition of the word is: to err is human; to forgive is divine.

8: *To add emphasis*: Commas, and other punctuation marks, can be used for dramatic effect as well as for clarity. Compare the following examples:

> It was a dull, grey day and the rain was pouring down relentlessly.

> It was a dull, grey day and the rain was pouring down, relentlessly.

> It was a dull, grey day and the rain was pouring down – relentlessly.

In the second version, a slight touch of drama has been added to the relentlessness of the rain, which was simply part of the dullness of the day in the first version, while in the third version the relentlessness has been foregrounded in a way which suggests that a story is about to start.

Finally, here, once again, are those three unbreakable rules about how *not* to use the comma:

1: A single comma should never intervene between an adjective (or the final adjective in a series) and the noun or phrase it qualifies, though a pair of bracketing commas conceivably might.

2: A single comma should never intervene between a subject and its verb, though a pair of bracketing commas frequently does.

3: If you introduce the first of a pair of bracketing commas, you can't do without the second.

Apostrophe

When Carey first wrote *Mind the Stop*, back in 1958, he rightly felt that the rules for the use of the apostrophe were so simple and so widely understood that he could deal with the subject in a paragraph. He totally failed to foresee the recent cultural shift which has left even the editors of broadsheet newspapers confused and error-prone. So, if you too are confused, here are the rules. Simply memorize and obey.

Where you *do* use an apostrophe:

1: *Possessive nouns*: The apostrophe precedes the *s* in the possessive case of singular nouns and follows the *s* in the possessive case of plural ones. Thus, 'She is the cat's mother', while Tabitha Twitchit, the female parent of Tom Kitten and his sisters, is 'the cats' mother'. If in doubt, you can work out which is correct by turning the phrase around: 'She is the mother of the cat', while 'Tabitha Twitchit is the mother of the cats'. The important thing to remember is that the apostrophe follows the noun. It can never interpose its own body between a plural noun and its *s* for the very good reason that the *s* is part of the noun.

Plural nouns not ending in *s* are followed by an apostrophe *s*: thus, the women's rugby team.

The possessive case of some singular nouns ending in *s* is formed by adding just an apostrophe, while others need an apostrophe *s*. This is determined simply by euphony (i.e. what sounds right and is easiest to say). Thus, 'Moses' destruction of the golden calf', but 'Tess's murder of Alec D'Urberville'. People often write things such as 'Tess' murder' because they have internalized an over-rigid rule about possessives ending in *s*, so if in doubt you should ask yourself what you would naturally say and spell it accordingly.

2: *Omitted letters*: The apostrophe is also used in contractions (shortened forms of words or phrases) to indicate that letters are missing. Thus, it's = it is, can't = cannot, don't = do not, shan't = shall not, and so on.

Where you *don't* use an apostrophe:

1: *Possessive Pronouns*: Just remember that the possessive pronoun 'its' belongs in the same box as 'yours', 'hers', 'his' and 'theirs', and none of them needs an apostrophe. The only exception is one's, but then one just has to be different.

2: *Nervous plurals*: The nervous plural, also known as the green-grocer's plural, occurs when a writer is unsure how to spell the plural of something slightly tricky, like a decade, a proper name or a root vegetable, and attempts to solve the problem by shoving in a redundant apostrophe as a way of touching wood. So just remember, in the 1960s and 1970s the Sloanes kept up with the Joneses by eating neither potatoes nor swedes. Apostrophes, who needs them?

In addition to all the above, students of literature need to be aware that in poetry an apostrophe taking the place of an elided vowel or consonant signals that a word has been shortened to fit the metre of the line, while an accented vowel, or a diphthong in which one vowel is marked with the two little dots called a diaeresis, signals that a word has been lengthened for the same reason. The first example comes from Andrew Marvell's *Bermudas* and the second from John Milton's *On the Morning of Christ's Nativity*. The 'birds of calm' in the second example are halcyons, mythological birds which were believed to breed in nests floating on the sea at the time of the winter solstice. 'Halcyon days' were originally the fourteen mid-winter days when the halcyons charmed the waves and the winds into stillness.

> Where the remote Bermudas ride
> In th'ocean's bosom unespied . . .

> The winds with wonder whist
> Smoothly the waters kissed,
>   Whispering new joys to the mild ocëan,
> Who now hath quite forgot to rave,
> While birds of calm sit brooding on the charmèd wave.

Inverted commas

Inverted commas are also known as quote marks or speech marks, indicating that two of their main uses are to enclose quotations and direct speech. Just as with question marks and indirect questions, speech marks are not used for indirect speech.

> He cried aloud, 'We perished,' and then again, 'each alone'.[20]

> She murmured, dreamily, half asleep, how we perished, each alone.[21]

In addition, inverted commas are used to enclose the titles of subsections of books, with the title of the book itself indicated by italics, and you can also use them to enclose words and phrases which, for whatever reason, you don't want to 'own'.

One practical problem with inverted commas is what to do when, for instance, you are quoting a passage containing direct speech which is itself enclosed in inverted commas. There is more than one opinion about this (some of them more heated than the subject really deserves) but the practical solution, which is also the logical one, is to go for the option which minimizes the use of the shift key and use single quotes as a general rule, doubling them for quotations or direct speech within quotations: 'He rose and stood in the bow of the boat, very straight and tall, for all the world, James thought, as if he were saying, "There is no God," and Cam thought, as if he were leaping into space . . .'[22] The important thing to remember is not to use single quotes inside single quotes, or double inside double, as this can seriously confuse your reader.

Dash

A dash – can be used instead of a colon to precede a clarification or illustration, and a pair of dashes can be used instead of brackets to separate 'asides' from the main drift of your sentence. However, while you always need both halves of a pair of brackets, you only need a single dash if your 'aside' is immediately followed by a full stop. Unlike other punctuation marks, which follow immediately after the final letter of the preceding word and are themselves followed by a space, you need to leave a space both before and after a dash or it will turn into a hyphen. If you are using Word for Windows, a hyphen will actually *grow* into a dash – like a Japanese paper flower unfolding in water – provided you remember to leave those spaces fore and aft.

Hyphen

Hyphens, unlike dashes, need to fit snugly between the words they connect, without a space either before or after. The use of hyphens is often optional – the reader will not be confused whether you write paperback book or paper-back book, so it is simply a question of taste (though you may sometimes find that the taste of your computer spell check is different from your own). However, hyphens do present one small but intractable problem which is neatly summed up by Ernest Gowers in *The Complete Plain Words*:

> It seems natural to use a hyphen in 'hair-remover', but Fowler pointed out that 'superfluous hair-remover' can only mean a hair-remover nobody wants. Neither 'superfluous-hair remover' nor 'superfluous-hair-remover' is quite satisfactory, and some of us might settle for 'superfluous hair remover'. But it seems odd that the addition of the adjective should lead us to abandon the hyphen that is natural in the compound noun standing by itself. The truth is that there is no satisfactory answer.[23]

I'm afraid that I don't have a satisfactory answer to it either, except that, whatever else you do, you should try to avoid ambiguity. In the following example, the writer has decided to dispense with hyphens altogether, with confusing results:

> Bloom also daydreams in front of a spice and teashop.

Instead of picturing Bloom in front of a shop which sells both spice and tea, the reader is momentarily fooled into imagining him standing in front of 'a spice' (whatever that may be) and a teashop in the other sense of tearoom or café. Either 'a spice-and-tea shop' or 'a spice and tea shop' would have been a better solution.

Parentheses and Brackets

Round brackets: A pair of parentheses (round brackets), like a pair of dashes, can be used to enclose material which adds a definition, illustration or clarification to some part of the subject matter of your sentence without altering its syntax. By definition, the sentence should remain grammatically complete and unchanged if the parenthesis is removed. You need to take care that your reader is not prevented from following the drift of your argument by over-long or obtrusive parentheses, and you also need to make sure that the punctuation of the rest of your sentence remains just as it would be without the bracketed material. This may require you to put a comma or full stop immediately after the closing bracket, though the convention is that you don't instead put a comma immediately before the opening one. Any punctuation marks inside your brackets should belong to the bracketed material, while all the punctuation marks outside them should belong to the parent sentence:

> Lily Briscoe was unable to express her sympathy for Mr Ramsay, so instead she praised his 'beautiful boots'.

> Lily Briscoe was unable to express her sympathy for Mr Ramsay (due, at least in part, to his oppressive need for an emotional response from her), so instead she praised his 'beautiful boots'.

> Lily Briscoe was unable to express her sympathy for Mr Ramsay, so instead she praised his 'beautiful boots' (causing him to forget, at least for a moment, his oppressive need for an emotional response from her).

Square brackets can be used to enclose any changes you need to make to a quotation to get it to fit neatly into the context of your essay, thus making it clear to your reader exactly what liberties you have taken with the original text. Square brackets allow you to change 'she' into [Mrs Ramsay] or add a bit of explanatory detail:

> Mrs Ramsay [Virginia Woolf's mother Julia Stephen] having died rather suddenly the night before . . .[24]

They also enable you to shorten a passage, quoting only the parts which are relevant to the point you are making:

> 'He must have reached it,' said Lily Briscoe aloud, feeling suddenly completely tired out. [. . .] 'He has landed,' she said aloud. 'It is finished.'[25]

You need to make sure, though, that you don't distort the text through selective quotation, like one of those theatre posters on which a less than wholehearted review – 'While not the best Hamlet I have ever seen, this production is competently acted on the whole, apart from the lacklustre performance of Jane Smith as Ophelia' – is filleted into: THE BEST HAMLET I HAVE EVER SEEN – GUARDIAN.

Ellipsis

Ellipses are the three little dots used to indicate omissions from a quoted passage. If you miss out several lines of text, as in the example above, the ellipsis should be enclosed in square brackets; if you only miss out a word or two, the ellipsis on its own is sufficient:

> 'He must have reached it,' said Lily . . . feeling suddenly completely tired out.

An ellipsis at the end of a quotation indicates that you have broken off before the end of a sentence, while in a romantic novel it indicates that a discreet veil of silence is being drawn over the heroine's bliss as she sinks into the hero's manly embrace.

Paragraphs

It is important to remember that paragraphing, far from being a convention requiring you to divide your essay into shorter units of more or less the same length, is actually an important way of signalling the progressive stages of your argument. Ernest Gowers puts this brilliantly in *The Complete Plain Words* when he says that 'the paragraph is essentially a unit of thought, not of length'.[26]

And finally, here is an anonymous puzzle poem which demonstrates how crucial punctuation can be, despite appearing to have none. Depending on where you mentally supply the punctuation marks, it is either an inventory of impossible marvels or a sober list of things which we mostly fail to be astonished by when perhaps we should be. A pismire, by the way, is an ant.

> I saw a peacock with a fiery tail
> I saw a blazing comet drop down hail

I saw a cloud wrappèd with ivy round
I saw an oak creep on along the ground
I saw a pismire swallow up a whale
I saw the sea brim full of ale
I saw a Venice glass five fathom deep
I saw a well full of men's tears that weep
I saw red eyes all of a flaming fire
I saw a house bigger than the moon and higher
I saw the sun at twelve o'clock at night
I saw the Man that saw this wondrous sight.

Grammar

It is not possible to include a complete English reference grammar in a book of this kind, so this section deals with grammatical points, both ancient and modern, which students (and other serious writers) often find particularly confusing.

agreement of verbs   Verbs should agree with their subjects rather than with the nearest possible noun or pronoun.

> The typical Jane Austen heroine, such as the independent-minded Lizzie Bennet, the wilfully passionate Marianne Dashwood and the proud and opinionated Emma Woodhouse, are not at all like Fanny Price, the subdued and timid heroine of *Mansfield Park*.

It is not Lizzie, Marianne and Emma but 'the typical Jane Austen heroine' who is being contrasted with Fanny, so the sentence should read:

> The typical Jane Austen heroine . . . is not at all like Fanny Price . . .

dangling modifiers   A dangling modifier is a phrase or clause with no grammatical subject of its own which dangles awkwardly from your sentence, often desperately trying to attach itself to some inappropriate subject:

> Having summoned up a vanished world of devout (if problematized) religious observance in the opening section, the

reader's eye is drawn to a sudden change in the verse form of the poem.

This seems an extraordinarily ambitious conjuring trick for the reader's eye to have pulled off – but of course it is not really the reader's eye but the absent poet who has done the summoning up. Put him back into the sentence and it makes grammatical sense:

> Heaney having summoned up a vanished world of devout (if problematized) religious observance in the opening section, the reader's eye is drawn to a sudden change in the verse form of the poem.

double negatives   In written English, double negatives don't intensify each other, they cancel each other out. If I feel a not undue concern, I am duly concerned.

grammar checks   While computer spell checks are helpful when you know how to use them, computer grammar checks were designed to improve the business correspondence of widget salesmen and are worse than useless to serious writers of any kind. When I tested one out on a few masterpieces of English prose, it advised Jane Austen to avoid 'gender-specific expressions':

> It is a truth universally acknowledged that a single person, human being or individual in possession of a good fortune must be in want of a spouse . . .

It advised Virginia Woolf to avoid 'excessive use of the passive voice' and washed its hands of Henry James: his sentences were 'too long to process for grammatical structure'.

in to and into / on to and onto   'Into' and 'onto' are not simply alternative ways of spelling 'in to' and 'on to', as the following pairs of examples should make clear:

> The pumpkin turned into a coach.
> The coach turned in to the drive.

> He went onto the platform.
> She went on to greater things.

may and might   To become technical for a moment, 'may' and 'might' are the present and past tenses of a modal auxiliary verb, which means that – along with their companions 'can'/'could', 'shall'/'should', 'must', 'ought to' and 'used to' – they 'enable us to talk about things that are not facts, but about possibility, probability, certainty, uncertainty, permission and so on. This includes the future, which is unknown.'[27] The important point about 'may' and 'might' is that the consequences of the past are also sometimes unknown; traditionally, 'may' has been used to indicate uncertainty about whether or not something has happened and 'might' to indicate that something could have happened but didn't. This distinction has recently started to erode, with 'may' often being used for both situations, even by otherwise careful writers. The reason for trying to reverse this particular bit of cultural slippage has nothing to do with correctness and everything to do with accuracy. Look at the following examples and think about the likely effect of saying the second when you really mean the first:

> 'There's been a terrible accident. Your son might have been killed.' (It was a miracle that he escaped with cuts and bruises.)

> 'There's been a terrible accident. Your son may have been killed.' (The police are still trying to identify the bodies.)

my husband and I   The Queen's most famous phrase tends to arouse either a republican feeling that this construction must be elitist and absurd or a Hyacinth-Bucket-like desire to imitate it at all costs. You can test out the correctness of 'My husband and I have visited forty countries this year' by forcing Elizabeth to travel alone: 'I have visited forty countries this year.' She and Philip are joint subjects of the sentence, so she is right to say I. Conversely, 'The Queen shook hands with my husband and I' is incorrect because the loyal couple here are joint objects of the sentence. Its speaker would never say, 'The Queen shook hands with I.'

order of clauses   The order in which clauses or phrases appear in a sentence can make the difference between sense and nonsense, as is demonstrated by the example of the first-time father who attempted to buy a rattle for a baby with a bell inside.

prepositions   The fact that one phrase is a synonym for another does not necessarily mean that it can include the same preposition. T. S. Eliot can be accused *of* misogyny in *The Waste Land*, but he can only be criticized *for* it. Sometimes, using the wrong preposition can create a different and unintended meaning, as in this example from the ITV News: 'the hospital was put on standby for an admission by the Prime Minister.[28]' In fact the hospital was awaiting not a statement on the NHS but the possible admission *of* the Prime Minister, who was feeling unwell.

shall and will   The distinction here is between a simple future tense − I / we shall, you (singular and plural) will, he / she / it / they will − and an expression of intention, in which 'shall' is replaced by 'will', and vice versa. That is why the bride and groom say 'I will' rather than 'I shall', and why the Fairy Godmother says, 'Cinderella, you *shall* go to the ball.' Robert Burns uses both the first person plural and the third person plural in *Robert Bruce's March to Bannockburn*[29] (the italics are his).

> By Oppression's woes and pains!
> By your Sons in servile chains!
> We will drain our dearest veins,
>   But they *shall* be free!

Expressions of intention don't get much more determined than that.

Nowadays, the first person 'shall' of the future tense is often replaced by 'I / we will', but, except in some dialect usages, it is still the case that 'you shall' is an order and 'he / she / it / they shall' is an expression of intention. So while you can certainly say, 'In this essay, I will discuss Virginia Woolf's last novel, *Between the Acts*', since that is your intention, if you say, 'this essay shall discuss Virginia Woolf's *Between the Acts*' you risk giving the impression that, but for your firm hand on the reins, the essay might have chosen to discuss Enid Blyton's *The Faraway Tree* instead.

they/them/their   The English language lacks a non-gender-specific singular personal pronoun, since it/its can be used of living beings only if they are plants, animals or, at a pinch, babies. Historically, he/him/his was assumed to 'contain' she/her, just as the word 'man' was assumed to 'contain' 'woman':

> Everyone is entitled to his share.

By the 1970s, however, women were pointing out with increasing force that, however grammatically inclusive it might be, this convention had the political effect of linguistically excluding women from all but purely female areas of life, and sometimes even from those. Casey Miller and Kate Swift, in their witty and polemical book *Words and Women*, quote the wording of a bill proposed in 1975 by the State of Connecticut:

> at least twenty-four hours before any abortion is performed in the state, the person who is to have such abortion shall receive counselling . . . concerning his decision to have such abortion.[30]

While the supposedly inclusive man/men was, after some initial ridicule, easily replaced by the genuinely inclusive person/people (or persons), enabling chairmen of both sexes to become chairpersons, and mankind experienced no real difficulty in becoming humankind, the lack of an appropriate singular pronoun led to the unwieldy constructions 'he or she' and 'his or her':

> Everyone is entitled to his or her share.

Though this may seem a fairly recent problem, caused by the success of the women's movement, attempts to address it actually date back to the mid nineteenth century. In 1859 the American composer Charles Converse coined the word 'thon' (a contraction of 'that one'), which survived, in dictionaries at any rate, for a hundred years but never became part of general usage, which is why we don't say:

> Everyone is entitled to thon's share.

In the 1970s, unsuccessful linguistic experiments of this kind multiplied; Miller and Swift, writing in 1976, list '*E, hesh, po, tey, ve, xe,* and *jhe*' among 'recent proposals'.[31] The socialist writer Edith Nesbit (1858–1924) opted for a simpler solution in her children's books to stress the equality of girls and boys in the families she described:

> Everyone got its legs kicked and its feet trodden on in the
> scramble to get out of the carriage.[32]

However, this usage (though logical and neat) sounded intentionally comic, and any Edwardian child who imitated it was presumably soon corrected.

More recently, writers have quietly begun to adopt, and editors to accept, a usage which in fact dates back to the sixteenth century:

> Everyone is entitled to their share.

Though the use of they/them/their in the singular as well as the plural is not yet universally accepted, the distinguished lexicographer R. W. Burchfield wryly admitted in *The New Fowler's Modern English Usage* that 'the process now seems irreversible'. No doubt late seventeenth-century grammarians felt the same regret as they watched the irreversible process through which the pronoun 'you' successfully saw off 'thou' and 'ye' (of which more in the following section). However, words don't belong to lexicographers and grammarians, they belong to the great all-inclusive mass of speakers and writers who alone determine how language is transformed over time. Everyone is entitled to their share, and if you can't beat them, join them.

thou / thee   Studying literature involves becoming familiar not only with contemporary uses of language but also with older ones, including now obsolete grammatical forms – although in fact the use of 'thee' has not completely died out even today. 'Thou', with its objective case 'thee' and its possessive case 'thy' or 'thine', is a second person singular pronoun, the plural form being 'ye' or 'you'. It could be used, like the French *tu*, either to signal that the person being addressed was a social inferior (who would therefore reply using the respectful plural pronoun) or that both speakers were in an equal and intimate relationship (hence its continued poetic use, especially in love poems, long after it had largely disappeared from everyday speech). Since 'thou' was used to inferiors, it was also possible to employ it as a deliberate insult. There is even a verb 'to thou', which Shakespeare's Sir Toby Belch uses in *Twelfth Night* when urging Sir Andrew Aguecheek to challenge the disguised Viola to a duel: 'Taunt him with the licence of ink. If thou thou'st him some thrice, it shall not be amiss . . .'[33] The irony here is that Toby's use of 'thou' in addressing Sir Andrew himself, which is meant to pass for bonhomie, expresses exactly the same kind of contempt for the man who is his dupe rather than his friend – while his companion implicitly confesses his own inferiority, even as he tries to retain his dignity, by addressing Toby with the more formal 'you'.

The use of 'thou' when addressing God may have been at least partly due to a desire to stress the oneness of the Trinity. However, once 'thou' fell out of normal speech its significance underwent a radical change and it became a heightened and formal pronoun rather than an intimate one, making its continued use in hymns and sermons seem like a particular mark of respect. This semantic shift has ironic implications for the other users of the verb 'to thou' (and the associated verb 'to thee'), the Quakers or members of the Religious Society of Friends. Their founder George Fox declares in his *Journal* that

> when the Lord sent me forth into the world, he forbade me to put off my hat to any, high or low; and I was required to 'thee' and 'thou' all men and women, without any respect to rich or poor, great or small.

Despite the fact that by the mid seventeenth century the use of 'thou' was already in decline, Fox accordingly insisted on using it to all addressees, regardless of rank, as an essential part of the 'plain speech' adopted as an assertion of universal equality. This usage is illustrated by the almost certainly apocryphal story about the Quaker William Penn (the founder of Pennsylvania) who attended an audience with Charles II where he was surprised to see the king take off his hat. 'Why dost thou doff thy hat to me, Friend Charles? Thou seest that I do not doff mine to thee.' 'Ah,' replied the king, 'but it is the custom here, Friend Penn, that only one man should go hatted at a time.' Once the pronoun 'you' (originally the accusative of the formal or plural 'ye') began to be used to 'all men and women, without any respect to rich or poor, great or small', the retention of 'thou' and 'thee', far from demonstrating egalitarianism, had the effect of setting its users apart from the wider community. Those Friends who still use 'plain speech' today tend to do so mainly to family members, and even this restricted use is obsolete in Britain and becoming increasingly rare in America, though appropriately one place where it still survives is Philadelphia, the city to which William Penn gave a name meaning 'brotherly love'.[34]

One oddity of Quaker usage is described by Selma Sheldon (born 1924):

> Thee is supposed to be the object form of the word, and yet Quakers in my day have always used it as subject as well. Thus, 'Thee is looking lovely today.' I never heard plain friends (as we call the theeing folk) use the word 'thou'.[35]

This substitution of 'thee' for 'thou' may originally have been due to the greater strength of nonconformism in the north of England, where the dialect forms 'tha' and 'thee' are still in use today.

'Thou' was used with its own present and past tense verb forms, which were usually accompanied (in the present tense at least) by a distinction between third person singular and third person plural:

> To be: thou art, thou wert, he / she / it is
> To do: thou dost, thou didst, he / she / it doth
> To have: thou hast, thou hadst, he / she / it hath
> To say: thou sayest, thou saidst, he / she / it sayeth
> To see: thou seest, thou sawst, he / she / it seeth

to stand, to sit and to lie   In informal speech, the present participles of the verbs 'to stand' and 'to sit' are often replaced by the past participle: people say 'I was stood' or 'I was sat' instead of 'I was standing' or 'I was sitting'. The problem with imitating this usage in your essay is that using the past participle turns an active verb into a passive one, implying that the standing or sitting is caused by some outside agency:

> The milk bottles were stood on the doorstep (by the milkman).

> The baby was sat in his highchair (by his mother).

In the case of the verb 'to lie', if you are laid (as opposed to lying) on the bed it is because someone else has put you there, and if you are laying on the bed you should be doing it in the hen-house instead.

verbing nouns   The American Secretary of State General Alexander Haig, famous for calling a lie 'a terminological inexactitude', is also popularly credited with having said that there's no noun that can't be verbed. If so, he was quite right – the process which linguists call conversion (the use of one part of speech as another) has always been one of the ways in which the English language has adapted over time, enabling us to talk about chairing a meeting, elbowing someone out of the way, or silencing an inconvenient witness. However, these coinages tend to be greeted with derision when they first appear, so – unless you are making a deliberate point which you know your reader will be able to pick up – it is sensible not to imitate General Haig's cavalier way with the English language.

who, whom, whose   Whom is the objective case and whose the possessive case of the relative pronoun 'who'. In speech, and in informal writing, 'whom' is nowadays usually replaced by 'who'. This is increasingly seen as acceptable even in more formal writing, but, conversely, it is still a solecism (though a very easy one to commit) to replace 'who' by 'whom'. You can avoid this by turning your phrase or sentence around to check that 'whom' is indeed the object, not the subject, of the relevant verb. For example, 'Mr Ramsay, whom Lily Briscoe saw as unappreciative of his wife . . .' is correct, because Mr Ramsay is the object of the verb 'saw': Lily Briscoe saw *him* as unappreciative of his wife. However, 'Mr Ramsay, whom Lily Briscoe thought behaved selfishly to his wife . . .' is incorrect because Mr Ramsay is the subject of the verb 'behaved': Lily Briscoe thought that *he* behaved selfishly to his wife.

Further reading

You will have rightly deduced that grammar is a much larger and more complex subject than punctuation. It is also one on which you can find any number of books, variously addressed to school pupils of all ages, non-native speakers, and students (not to mention professors) of linguistics, as well as to the serious adult apprentice writer. You may have a use for any or all of the above. If you are a non-native speaker, try A. J. Thomson and A. V. Martinet, *A Practical English Grammar* (Oxford, 1986) or John Eastwood's *Oxford Guide to English Grammar* (Oxford, 1994). If you feel that your grammar is so rudimentary that you need to begin with a school textbook, try David Crystal's *Rediscover Grammar* (Longman, 1988). Students of English literature as well as English language could profit from Dennis Freeborn's *From Old English to Standard English: A Course Book in Language Variation Across Time* (Macmillan, 1992), which is full of interesting illustrative material which makes it clear why writers in different historical periods used language in such different ways. However, if, as a serious adult apprentice writer, you want a comprehensive user's guide to the English language, you would be well advised to acquire, and attentively study, Sidney Greenbaum's *An Introduction to English Grammar* (Longman, 1991) This isn't particularly cheap, but it is eminently the kind of book you could ask a grandparent to give you for Christmas.

For spot answers to particular linguistic problems, you might also want to consult Eric Partridge, *Usage and Abusage: A Guide to Good English*, revised by Janet Whitcut (Penguin, 1994), while *The New Fowler's Modern English Usage*, revised by R. W. Burchfield (Oxford, 1996), though it too is not cheap, is a compact encyclopaedia of linguistic information and merits a permanent place on every serious professional writer's bookshelf.

If you need additional help with punctuation, G. V. Carey's *Mind The Stop: A Brief Guide to Punctuation* (Penguin) is still one of the best books on the subject. First published in 1939 and revised in 1958, it has deservedly remained in print ever since. As well as giving you wise, clear and genial advice, it offers a glimpse of a vanished world in the anthology of brief quotations which illustrate the various points. Alternately, another old but deservedly enduring guide, Ernest Gowers' *The Complete Plain Words* (revised by Sidney Greenbaum and Janet Whitcut: Penguin, 1987), contains a very useful chapter on punctuation which is a model of lucid exposition. Both Carey and Gowers are concerned with imparting a professional skill to intelligent adult learners and are refreshingly free from over-prescriptiveness or that hysteria about falling standards which often fogs the subject of punctuation today, so I would recommend their solid advice in preference to that of more recent (and sometimes more entertaining) writers.

Chapter 9

Foreign languages and literature

Se ciapa più mosche co 'na gozza de miele che co 'na bote de asedo.

You can catch more flies with a drop of honey than with a barrel of vinegar.

Venetian proverb

Languages without Mr Casaubon

Without language it is impossible fully to engage in human life, yet every language contains within its idioms and grammatical structures a complex set of largely unexamined cultural assumptions which both defines and limits the speaker's sense of what human life actually consists of. Being able to move between languages helps us to question those assumptions, and thus to begin to understand other cultures from the basis of shared linguistic experience. In other words, learning a new language (or improving your grasp of one you have already started to master) not only enables you to read new books and talk to new people, it also offers the exciting possibility of an expanded world view and fresh ways of thinking and feeling. All too often, though, even people who got high marks in school language exams, let alone those who got low ones, are held back from adult language-learning by the disabling belief that they are 'no good at languages'.

In fact, of course, being good at languages is a universal human attribute which only extreme misfortune (such as a stroke which disables the language centres of the brain) is able to destroy. In multilingual communities or families, every child, regardless of its IQ, grows up fluent in more than one language. However, while almost everyone is good at languages, that does not mean that we are all equally good at being on the receiving end of language tuition, as

George Eliot vividly illustrates in a famous scene in *Middlemarch*. Here Eliot's heroine, the naively idealistic Dorothea Brooke, who has just got engaged to an elderly clergyman under the misguided impression that 'the really delightful marriage must be that where your husband was a sort of father, and could teach you even Hebrew, if you wished it',[1] is sitting down with her fiancé for her first Greek lesson:

> Mr Casaubon consented to listen and teach for an hour together, like a schoolmaster of little boys, or rather like a lover, to whom a mistress's elementary ignorance and difficulties have a touching fitness. Few scholars would have disliked teaching the alphabet under such circumstances. But Dorothea herself was a little shocked and discouraged at her own stupidity, and the answers she got to some timid questions about the value of Greek accents gave her a painful suspicion that here indeed there might be secrets not capable of explanation to a woman's reason.[2]

The secret poor Dorothea is being excluded from, as George Eliot knows only too well though the twenty-first century reader may not, is one that the erudite Mr Casaubon is unwilling to confess even to himself, let alone to the young lady he intends to marry, since it concerns a significant gap in the great male edifice of classical scholarship. The accents in classical Greek, which were not invented until the third century BC as an aid to reading the great poetry of the past, were a way of indicating musical pitch. Not only is this system alien to English speakers, who have a language accented by stress rather than pitch, but no one really knows what it sounded like in practice. As Donald J. Mastronarde forcefully puts it, in his *Introduction to Attic Greek*:

> Although scholars can deduce how the tonal accent worked on single words and short phrases that were treated as an accented unit, there is no way to discover how the accents sounded in longer utterances, and it is therefore idle (as well as very difficult) for the beginner to attempt a tonal rendering of Greek accents.[3]

In fact Dorothea has been triply cheated. Not only has she been left with the impression that she is ignorant and stupid in being unable to grasp what Mr Casaubon is unable to teach, she has also been deprived by him of the two essential components of successful adult language learning: the self-confidence which comes from taking control of your own language acquisition and the pleasure which comes from treating your chosen language not as a formidable and daunting task through which you have to be guided but as a passionate hobby on which you enjoy lavishing time and effort. Instead of delighting in the beauty and elegance of the Greek alphabet and taking pride in her determination to master it, Dorothea has been infantilized and put down, not only by the real Mr Casaubon but also by the inner one who does his insidious best to convince each of us that we are 'no good at languages'.

It is instructive to compare Dorothea's unhappy language-learning experience with that of a much younger and sassier George Eliot heroine, Maggie Tulliver in Book Two of *The Mill on the Floss*. When Maggie, who is being reluctantly home-educated in the domestic arts, visits her brother Tom at boarding-school, she is fascinated by his Latin grammar book and convinced that she could easily teach herself this new and enticing language. She rapidly discovers some 'mysterious sentences snatched from an unknown context'[4] in translation at the back of the book and wonders who wrote them and why – scandalizing her much less academically able brother, who has dimly and glumly intuited what Roland Barthes was later to spell out in *Mythologies*: that any apparently intriguing sentence that a schoolboy encounters in a Latin grammar book is there only to convey the 'impoverished' message, 'I am a grammatical example'.[5] The episode ends with one of the most crushing male put-downs in English literature, as Tom's headmaster declares that girls have 'a great deal of superficial cleverness: but they couldn't go far into anything. They're quick but shallow.'[6] However, Maggie's language discoveries have left Tom aware for the first time that 'there had once been people upon the earth who were so fortunate as to know Latin without learning it through the medium of the Eton Grammar'.[7]

While George Eliot is concerned in both these episodes with the ways in which nineteenth-century young women were thwarted in their desire to share the educational opportunities available to their brothers, she is also making a sharp point about language learning. It is Maggie's eager intellectual curiosity and her confident belief in her own abilities which brings Latin alive for her, while Dorothea's humble conviction that she needs a husband who is also a father (male authority squared) to instruct her in even the rudiments of classical Greek provides the psychological excuse Mr Casaubon needs to continue to hoard the dead language which he is in any case unable to share because for him it has never lived.

Real-life language learning

While the language teaching you received at school is unlikely to have matched the painfulness of Dorothea's experience, whole-class learning is not always the best way to acquire a language, and is often accompanied by well-meaning assumptions which actually hold you back – whether it is the old-fashioned idea that you need to master the whole of grammar before embarking on anything as sinfully pleasurable as reading a book or the new-fangled notion that verbs are so difficult that their tenses need to be doled out with painstaking slowness, leaving you stranded in the present without a subjunctive to your name and unable to read a book if you tried. Instead I want to offer you a different method, which could be described as real-life language learning.

In classroom language learning, the most important factor is receptiveness to the teacher's programme, and the proof of success is getting good marks in a test (conversely, the proof of failure is getting bad ones). In real-life language learning, the most important factor, especially for adult learners, is commitment, and the proof of success can be anything from managing to buy a cup of coffee to grasping the contents of a film or book. Most important of all, there is no such thing as failure; indeed, learning from your mistakes is a crucial part of real-life language acquisition. Since you will be making your chosen language your own, you need to make the learning process your own as well – so feel free to experiment by adapting the advice which follows in any way which seems helpful. Every language has its own difficulties, beauties and puzzles and there is no single blueprint for how to tackle them all.

However, there is just one rule to bear in mind before you start: learning a language is like learning a musical instrument. Just as half an hour's music practice a day is better than a blockbuster session the evening before your flute or violin lesson, while two or three hours a day enables you to become a serious musician, so daily practice will help to consolidate your language skills. This need not take the form of slogging over grammatical exercises (as you will see, you won't be doing much of that anyway). Watching a film, reading a detective novel, making sense of an opera libretto, going on holiday to a place where your language is spoken and even studying a menu are all ways of increasing and reinforcing your knowledge of a foreign language.

Speaking and listening

If, unlike Dorothea, you have chosen to study a modern language, you need to have it in your ears and in your mouth from the very beginning, even if your main purpose in learning is to improve your reading skills. This means starting with language tapes. The BBC produces excellent and affordable taped language courses which are available in a wide range of languages, with back-up books and Learning Zone television programmes, all of which you should take advantage of. (Don't try to economize by buying one of those tapes of phrases for travellers which teach you how to announce, with unnatural distinctness, that you would like a boiled, or alternatively a fried, egg.) Listening to native speakers enables you to master the things – such as word order and intonation – which make up the tune the language is sung to, or rather the repertoire of tunes, since there is no single way of speaking French or German or Russian or Turkish any more than there is a single way of speaking English. Speaking your chosen language, even in conversation with a cassette recorder, enables you to begin to take possession of it and to build up an active vocabulary and also gives you familiarity with what you will later discover to be some useful basic grammar. (Even knowing how to say 'I would like a boiled egg' enables you to practise one of the uses of the conditional tense.) You don't need to worry about whether you sound like a native speaker yourself – you won't, unless you are an outstanding mimic – but neither should you feel abashed about putting a bit of French exuberance, Gaelic lilt or Spanish fire into your pronounciation. Language is about communication, and your aim, as a speaker of your new language, is to be understood, not to radiate nervous correctness or Anglophone embarrassment.

In fact, learning to listen is far more difficult than learning to speak. Trying to comprehend a foreign language is like being hard of hearing – even things which you would understand straight away if they were written down can defeat you if you are unable to disentangle the sense from the sounds. The more listening you do (enjoying the tune the language is sung to, even if you can't always follow the words) the more quickly you will begin to overcome this problem. Don't just rely on your language tapes to help you build up your skills as a listener, though playing them repeatedly, until you know, without even having to think about it, exactly what is being said, is a very useful way to start. (You can do this while you tidy your bedroom, take a bath, cook the supper and do the washing up – though, unless your house-mates or relatives also want to learn Japanese, a Walkman with head-phones is essential equipment for combining total language immersion with domestic harmony.) You should also start exploring as many other ways as possible of hearing and speaking your new language.

You can learn enough from two or three intensive weeks spent with a taped language course to enable you to buy a meal or a drink, ask the way, and have a simple conversation about who you are and where you come from, enabling you to use your new language in a country (or even a café) where it is spoken. You may well be able to find an overseas student studying at your university who would be happy to spend a few hours a week helping you improve your conversational Arabic or Portuguese in return for reciprocal help with conversational English. (If the resulting friendship becomes warm enough, you may get the chance to test out the old Italian proverb which says that languages are learnt best in bed.) Look out for television programmes about any aspect of any country where your language is spoken – and cross your fingers that any native speakers interviewed are subtitled rather than dubbed. If you enjoy music, look for CDs of folk-songs, pop songs or even operas in your new language (especially ones which include a leaflet with the words) and learn to sing in your language as well as to speak it. Music has a mnemonic effect (it is much easier to remember the words of a song than the words of a poem), so this is an excellent way of making vocabulary stick in your head. One helpful thing, if you are trying to improve your language comprehension, is that it is much easier to acquire a passive vocabulary (words you recognize and understand when you meet them) than an active one (words which are on the tip of your tongue when you need them).

A particularly valuable language aid, especially once you have begun to feel confident about your grasp of basic vocabulary and grammar, and one which spans the gap between listening and reading, is provided by the multilingual options which come with many DVDs. Look for a film you know well and enjoy which has subtitles or a dubbed soundtrack in your chosen language. Most useful of all are those which have both, plus English subtitles for the hard of hearing. This enables you to listen to your film in English while reading the French or German subtitles, then listen to it in French or German while following the English subtitles, then listen to it in French or German without the aid of subtitles. (Don't try to do all this in a single evening, or when your house-mates are trying to watch the rugby. Real-life language learning can easily become obsessive.) While you obviously can't look up all the difficult words in the subtitles at the same time as watching a film, scribbling down a few key ones to look up later is a useful addition to the other kinds of reading which will accompany your experiments with speaking and listening.

Reading

It is only through reading that you can build up an effective vocabulary (most people use a surprisingly small lexicon in everyday speech) and the same thing goes for the ability to make sense of complex sentence structures, so, in addition to speaking and listening to your new language, you need to start learning to read it as quickly as possible. Aristotle rightly said that the things we have to learn to do, we learn by doing,[8] and fortunately there is one sure-fire way of learning to read in a foreign language – actually doing it for real, starting with children's picture books and gradually working your way up, via magazines and detective novels, to major works of literature. The best way to learn the grammar and vocabulary of your chosen language is in the context of this kind of real-life reading. You won't need to memorize tables of verbs or lists of word-meanings, and neither will you need to do grammatical exercises unless you actually enjoy them (perversely enough, some people do). Instead, you will find yourself doing a formidable amount of looking things up and thinking about the structures of the language, with recognition and understanding taking the place of rote learning in enabling you to make sense of what is happening on the page. This is hard work, especially at the early picture book stage when you will be mastering most of the grammatical knowledge you will need later on, but it is hard work of a satisfyingly challenging kind; and repeated acts of recognition will eventually result in a much more secure and detailed grasp of grammar and vocabulary than anything you can achieve by laboriously learning lists of words off by heart.

In order to make a start, you need a suitable picture book (a translation of one you read and enjoyed as a child will give you a head start in making intelligent guesses) and you also need a bilingual dictionary, a reference grammar and a book of irregular verbs. Finding your picture book is easy if you get the chance to visit a country where your language is spoken (in which case, if you can afford it, you should stock up on a small pile of paperbacks for readers between five and fifteen), and it is possible that your university library includes children's books among its resources for language learners. Failing that, you will need to make use of Grant and Cutler's foreign language bookshop[9] or Amazon.co.uk. Language learners are traditionally advised to start with a translation into their chosen language of Antoine de Saint-Exupéry's *The Little Prince* (or the original, *Le petit prince*, if that language is French) but, even if you enjoy existential whimsy, this is quite a difficult text for beginners. I would recommend choosing something by Beatrix Potter, who has been translated into French, German, Latin, Italian, Norwegian, Spanish, Swedish and Welsh and quite possibly other languages besides. Though her books were intended for the very young, they are written in quite sinewy and (considering their audience) even demanding prose which has nothing in common with the bland and repetitive contents of present-day early readers, so they have more than enough in the way of interesting vocabulary and grammar to get you started. Really, though, any reasonably short and straight-forward book which takes your fancy will do, especially if it has illustrations. If you choose something more difficult, you will simply have to spend a bit longer making sense of it.

Choosing your tool-kit of language books is something you need to put a bit of care and research into, as you will still be using them long after you have put *Pierre Lapin* or *Geremia Pescatore* behind you. Your bilingual dictionary needs to be as detailed and capacious as possible, but not so large and heavy that you can't comfortably consult it as you read. Pocket or gem dictionaries suitable for tourists on holiday are of no use at all to serious linguists like you, since they don't give you anything like the complete range of possible meanings of even the small number of words that they contain. You are looking for something at least the size of the *Concise Oxford English Dictionary* and similarly packed with information. The reference section of your university library should give you the chance to compare the contents and user-friendliness of various possibilities. Good dictionaries are not cheap, so this is something worth looking for in second-hand bookshops, though don't buy one which is seriously out of date.

Your book of irregular verbs should be easier to find, since there is an excellent series called *201 Arabic Verbs* (and on down the alphabet to Vietnamese) published by Barron's Educational Series Inc. These helpfully include the whole of every tense of the 201 verbs (not just the irregular bits) and also include sample regular verbs plus a conjugated English verb to show you what the names of the tenses mean.

The third item in your tool-kit, a reference grammar, should include all the grammatical information (such as definite and indefinite articles; plurals of nouns and adjectives; personal, possessive and relative pronouns; conjugations of verbs and uses of tenses) which you will need in order to master your chosen language. It will be much more useful if it is arranged by topics rather than as a graduated language course complete with grammatical exercises. However, even the language-course kind of grammar book can be useful if you can't find anything better, provided it has a good index and you don't mind dipping about in it to find the information you need. (The grammatical exercises will do you no harm if you like that sort of thing – and ignoring them will do you no harm either if you don't.) You will probably find that your bilingual dictionary also includes a skeleton grammar, which may be useful for cross-checking.

Having assembled your chosen text and your language tool-kit, it is time to start reading. You will actually be reading your picture book three times, in three different ways. The first time, you simply read the way you did as a child, making sense of the text as best you can with the help of the pictures and guessing the words you don't know. You will discover (if you have forgotten what it was like the first time round) that small children have to put a lot of effort and lateral thinking into decoding a simple text. Keep your dictionary shut and don't cheat by looking at the English version of the story (if you have one). If the adult in you wants to make notes, either about what you think you have guessed right or what you need to check, do it in a separate notebook, not on the pages of the picture book itself. You need to keep that pristine for the third stage in the process.

The second reading, which will probably take you quite some time and may well need several sessions, is the one where you look up the meaning of every word and phrase, as well as identifying all the parts of speech and tracking down the person and tense of every verb. The following section on 'Vocabulary and grammar' will give you some suggestions about how to do this. At this second stage you also get the chance to discover how intelligent your stage one guesses were. If you find that there is some linguistic riddle to which you can't work out the answer however hard you try, don't worry about it. You are sure to encounter the same problem again later in some other context when your command of the language and your lateral thinking skills have increased enough for you to solve it.

Finally, put away your dictionary, verb book and reference grammar and read the story for a third time, doing your best not to translate it into English in your head but to let the words on the page speak to you directly. (This takes a bit of practice, but it is an essential skill to learn if you want to become a really fluent reader.) Once again you will be reading like a child, but this time like a French or Italian or Swedish child, for whom *lapin* or *coniglio* or *kanin* doesn't mean 'the English word rabbit' but is the name of a thing in the world, a small wild creature with long ears and a fluffy white tail. Don't be surprised if, despite all your hard work, you find that there are words or phrases which you still have to guess. On average, for a new word to become securely part even of your passive vocabulary, you need to encounter it at least fifty times – a process you have already made a substantial start on with all that rereading and looking things up. And at least this time round your intelligent guesses are almost certain to be correct.

While it would obviously be much too labour-intensive to go through this three-stage process with everything you read, it is helpful to repeat it with quite a lot of children's books, gradually moving on to longer and more challenging ones. Collections of folk-tales are also a useful source of early reading material. Once you feel ready to tackle a full-length book, you can start to build up your lateral thinking skills by doing free reading in your chosen language – simply reading the way you would normally read a detective novel or a thriller rather than a literary text. Indeed, a detective novel or thriller is ideal for this kind of reading (the works of Agatha Christie and Georges Simenon have been translated into a multitude of different languages) but so is any book which takes your fancy, provided you can make at least partial sense of the first page. Browse along the bookshop or library shelves until you find something you like the look of.

Once you have found a suitable book, just open it and start reading. Don't worry if there are a lot of things you don't understand provided you can begin to make out the gist of the story. Look up only those key words which will help you to make sense of a baffling paragraph or plot detail. This kind of reading is like feeling your way through a dark wood – it takes you a bit of time to get your night vision, but once you start to glimpse the outlines of what

surrounds you it becomes easier and easier to find your way. It does
need quite a lot of concentration, though, so read little but often,
stopping as soon as you begin to flag. If you are someone who likes
to have a bedside book, it is a good idea to do half an hour or so of
free reading every night before you go to sleep. If you combine your
free reading with a page of close reading, using your language
tool-kit, at least once a week, you will soon start to increase both
your comprehension and your reading speed. Choose pages which
will help you to judge whether your guesses about the story are
correct. The more books you read in this way, the better your
language skills will become. You may find, as you tackle each new
text, that the opening pages are unexpectedly difficult. This is
because you have got used to the idiolect (the personal language
sub-set) of the author of the previous book. Each new author will
broaden your horizon, adding his or her own contribution to your
growing vocabulary of words and idioms.

It goes without saying that you should also read anything else in
your chosen language which comes your way, from magazines and
newspapers (which can often be found in railway-station bookstalls)
to the small print on shampoo bottles and toothpaste tubes purchased
on holiday. You will be surprised to discover that all these things are
quite hard to make sense of. We are so used to the coded kinds of
English, often further complicated by puns, in jokes and topical
references, used in journalism and advertising that it is only when we
encounter foreign-language examples of the same thing that we realize
just how specialized they are. Unless you are trying to make sense of
a newspaper article about something important and under-reported
in the English media, there is no need to treat this kind of reading as
anything but fun. It will still help to make you a more fluent reader.

At this stage in the learning process, people taking language courses
are often advised to read parallel texts. Worthy anthologies with
titles such as *Modern Finnish Writing* or *Twenty-Five Hungarian Short
Stories* are published for this very reason. Books of this kind can give
you a sense of which writers in your chosen language you might
enjoy reading, but they won't teach you much Suomi or Magyar.
The English side of the page will irresistibly draw your eye,
destroying your night vision by shining a torch which shows you
the trees but blinds you to the wood. Even if you cover up the
English text, you will inevitably find yourself using it as a crib
instead of working out the vocabulary and grammar for yourself,
limiting both what you learn and what you retain from the reading

experience. Besides, you lose the buzz of achievement which comes from knowing that you can pick up a book in a foreign language and read it from cover to cover. Parallel texts are for wimps. Go for the hard stuff.

Latin and Greek

So far I have mainly been talking about modern languages, but of course the hardest kind of hard stuff – though well worth the effort for anyone with a passion for ancient history, archaeology or literature – is learning a language that nobody speaks any more. With no tapes, no films, no foreign holidays, no Ancient Greek or Roman pen pals, you are forced to fall back on books. In the case of Latin, you can replace the initial taped language course with something like Peter V. Jones and Keith C. Sidwell's *Reading Latin* course (Cambridge University Press) which includes a *Reading Latin Text*, and book of *Grammar, Vocabulary and Exercises* and *An Independent Study Guide*, or else go for a less earnest approach with *Latin for Dummies*. Early reading books are not a problem either. Start with Beatrix Potter's *Fabula De Petro Cuniculo*, translated by E. Peroto Walker, then move on to A. A. Milne, with Alexander Lenard's brilliant *Winnie Ille Pu* and Brian Staples's *Domus Anguli Puensis*. Of course you will also need a good Latin dictionary and reference grammar, as well as *201 Latin Verbs*. Latin grammar isn't easy, though certainly not beyond the powers of anyone with a real enthusiasm for the language, so be prepared to put in the hours. Reading real Roman texts traditionally starts with Caesar's *Gallic Wars*, but you might find the poems of Catullus more amusing – mostly short, often sexy or satirical or both, and occasionally obscene, they explode the myth that Latin is a dead language.

If, like poor Dorothea, the language you want to learn is classical Greek, you should start with the package which would have solved all her problems: the Joint Association of Classical Teachers Greek Course, *Reading Greek* (Cambridge University Press). This includes a student guide to grammar and vocabulary, an anthology of graduated texts, a book of *Teachers' Notes* (very useful to the serious adult learner), plus a cassette tape so that you can hear what the language may have sounded like. Useful as the *Reading Greek* course is, and despite the dearth of other early reading material, you don't need to confine yourself to it exclusively once you have learnt enough to start making sense of some short poems, or to try a little bit of the Greek New Testament (the language isn't exactly the same as classical Greek, but it is not as difficult either), or to tackle a page or two of one of Plato's Socratic dialogues (written in reader-friendly conversational form). Nor do you need to restrict yourself to the rather attenuated vocabulary lists, which only give you the definitions you need in order to make sense of the *Reading Greek* text passages. Get yourself a good dictionary.

It may seem too obvious to need saying, but your success in looking things up will entirely depend on your ability to remember the order of the letters in the Greek alphabet, just as your success in getting started on the language at all will depend on your learning the sounds and shapes of those letters in the first place. Both of these are feats of memory which small children achieve with the English alphabet in their primary school reception class, so don't come over all Dorothea Brooke about this. Just practise until you can do it. A card on which you have written the Greek letters and their names can be kept inside your dictionary as an *aide memoire* in the meantime.

Language lessons

Whether the language you are learning is ancient or modern, don't fail to take advantage of any language tuition your university has on offer, and certainly don't cut any language classes which you are required to take. You will probably find that language classes help to structure and reinforce your own language discoveries, and you may be lucky enough to encounter a really inspiring teacher. However, don't forget that a language which is in your mouth and eyes and ears belongs to you and you alone, and don't hand over custody of it to any teacher, however little he or she resembles Mr Casaubon, or limit your explorations by confining them to a course syllabus. Keep speaking, reading and listening to your chosen language, learn to think in it and even dream in it. As one particularly inspired language teacher used to say, the test of whether you have really made a language your own is whether you know it on your deathbed.

Vocabulary and grammar

Whether you are starting a language from scratch or already have an A-level in it, your approach to perfecting your grasp of vocabulary and grammar will help to determine how fluent a reader you eventually become. Your goal, of course, especially if you are studying the literature of your language at university, is to be able to read it like a native speaker – actually much easier, given that your passive vocabulary is likely to far outstrip your active one, than speaking it like a native. The secret, with both vocabulary and grammar, is to learn like an intelligent and literate adult, not like a schoolchild or a parrot. This is how you do it.

Don't be daunted if it seems like a lot of hard work. Remember, you'll be building up your knowledge bit by bit. Even five or ten minutes spent looking things up and thinking about what you have discovered will, if you do it regularly, help to get you nearer to your goal. If learning a language is like learning a musical instrument, then building up your knowledge of vocabulary and grammar is like practising your scales in order to be able to enjoy playing real music more fluently.

Vocabulary

Despite what they probably told you at school, memorizing lists of words and their meanings, virtuous though it may make you feel, is not really the best way of increasing your vocabulary. To start with, though you can acquire a basic lexicon of everyday words and phrases in this way, it isn't really possible to rote-learn all the words you will need to read even a fairly undemanding thriller. Nor are words which have been stripped of context and learnt off by heart always easy to recall when you need them. Only too many industrious language-learners have found that their laboriously acquired little foreign word hoard has melted away in the night like fairy gold, leaving them in the same shoes as James Joyce's Molly Bloom, who 'with care repeated, with greater difficulty remembered, forgot with ease, with misgiving rerememebered, rerepeated with error'.[10]

Most important of all, you only have to look at an entry or two in any large bilingual dictionary to see that words very seldom mean only one thing, and that the range of meanings of a word in one language is unlikely to map precisely on to those of any single word or phrase in another. To take a simple example, if you fix it into your head that the Italian word *bambino* means 'baby' while *ragazzo* means 'boy', you will be baffled to read about 'babies' climbing trees and decidedly elderly 'boys' hailing each other with a cheerful '*Ciao, ragazzi!*' Similarly, if you have got it into your head that the Italian preposition *di* 'means' the English preposition 'of', you will be puzzled when you find a small bambino saying about a larger one, '*mio fratello é più grande di me*' (my brother is bigger *than* me). In addition, idiomatic phrases can seldom be translated literally. Where an English mother might say that her skinny son is 'as thin as a rake', an Italian mamma might say instead, '*sembra un ragno*' (he's like a spider).

If you want to build up a sense of the range of meanings and idiomatic usages of any word in a foreign language, you need to be prepared to look it up in a sizeable dictionary, or even in several, reading through the relevant entry carefully to find the definition which best fits the context in which you found it. Once you have repeated the process often enough – and unless you have a photographic memory that is likely to be quite a number of times – that word, with all its charge of meanings, will be securely fixed in your head. You won't need to remember it any more than you need to remember the meanings of the English words you use every day. What is more, just like those English words, you won't need to translate or define it in order to understand it.

It goes without saying that this method really works only for people with a lively curiosity about words and their meanings. If you regard looking things up as a chore and skim mechanically through the dictionary entry until you light on the first definition which might conceivably fit, you will naturally learn very little. Conversely, if you approach the task with all the problem-solving enthusiasm of a real researcher, the small charge of pleasure which comes from being able to make sense of one more detail of the text you are reading will actually help you to retain the information you have discovered. There is experimental evidence that 'people remember neutral information better if they are in a good mood when they learn it'.[11] It is equally essential to know how to say, and thus to 'hear', the words you are looking up – few people find it easy to remember or even take in unpronounceable sequences of letters. You will need patience as well, and the self-confidence to realize that it is because language acquisition is a slow process, and not because you are slow on the uptake, that you have to keep on looking the same word up. Each time you do so, you will widen as well as deepen your eventual sense of its range of meanings, so none of your painstaking effort will go to waste.

However, there is one sort of word which you do need to commit to memory – although in order to remember exactly what it *doesn't* mean – and that is the sneakily deceptive kind known as a false friend. False friends are the words which we often don't bother to look up because we are so sure that they mean the same thing as some English word that they closely but misleadingly resemble. When you unmask one of these, it is a good idea to make a careful note of it so that it is less likely to fool you twice.

Grammar

Grammar is the scaffolding of language; it is what enables us to think as well as to communicate with others, since without it we would not be able to organize our words, and thus our ideas, into meaningful patterns. Children who, through extreme neglect or some other misfortune, are deprived of the human interaction needed to acquire speech (so called feral children) may later have little difficulty in building up quite large vocabularies but, having missed out on the early learning experiences which give us the ability to grasp grammatical structures, they never really learn to talk. In order to read or speak a foreign language, you need to be able to recognize the different parts of speech as they occur in the context of actual communication, not just as they appear in the grammar book. It is quite easy to learn things like the endings which indicate the gender and number of nouns and adjectives, but what do you do if, when you try to apply this knowledge to a page of prose, you are unable to pick out which words actually are nouns or adjectives, and which are other parts of speech with confusingly similar endings?

A useful way to train yourself to do this is to photocopy a few pages from an undemanding book in the language you are learning, choosing one which you also have in English translation. Now, using your English translation as a crib, go through your copied pages with a packet of coloured marker pens, highlighting the grammatical relationships between the words. Start by finding all the verbs on one page and marking them in yellow and then finding the subject of each verb and marking it in red. If your subject is a pronoun, you may find that it is actually contained within the verb, so underline your yellow verb in red. Then find the direct or indirect object of each verb, if it has one, and colour the direct objects green and the indirect ones blue. Make a key at the top of the page, with labelled coloured blobs, so that you remember what you were highlighting. Now take another copied page and mark all the nouns in red with their adjectives in pink and all the verbs in yellow with their adverbs in orange, not forgetting the key at the top of the page. Think carefully about any other grammatical relationships it might help you to highlight and make pages for them too. Now put away your English crib and go through your marked up pages one by one with the help of your language tool-kit. And finally go back to the book you photocopied the pages from and see if you can manage to read and understand the unmarked text. All this will probably take you several sessions. The closer together they are, the more likely you are to retain what you have learnt from one to the next, but take a break whenever your concentration and interest start to flag. Language learning is more successful the more you enjoy it, so treat this exercise as a difficult but engaging puzzle which you are trying to solve, not as a bit of dull but dutiful homework. A drop of honey is better than a barrel of vinegar at making grammar stick in your head.

A final happy thought about grammar is that the more of it you know the less of it you need to remember. While there is no end to the learning of vocabulary, if you persevere with your chosen language its grammar will eventually become second nature, at least as far as reading is concerned, and you will no longer even need to think about it.

Verbs

Verbs are the most important of all parts of speech and necessarily the most complicated, since they have to be varied enough to enable us to distinguish between what every grammatical person, number and gender (I, you singular, he, she, it, we, you plural and they) is, was, will be, has been, had been, could be, could have been, may or might or may be about to have been doing, or being at the receiving end of: loving and being loved, seeing and being seen, eating and being eaten. Not surprisingly, they are also the single feature of any language that learners fear most. In order to conquer that fear and live happily with verbs, you need both to understand the uses of the various tenses and to know how to identify all the parts of any and every verb you might encounter.

Traditionally, students were expected to master foreign verbs in much the same way as they were taught to master the twelve times table, by chanting sample specimens aloud. When I was at school, I was taught to memorize and recite the conjugations of Latin verbs, dutifully impressing on my memory the magical formula 'aMO, aMAS, aMAT, aMAmus, aMAtis, aMANT'. None of the rest of it stays with me, though my Latin is far more fluent now than it was in my schooldays. It was many years before I realized that by learning to emphasize the endings of the various parts of the verb I was also learning to mispronounce most of them. The accent in Latin falls on the second last syllable of the word if the vowel in that syllable is long, and on the previous one (provided the word has three or more syllables) if the vowel in the penultimate syllable is short. Scholars still argue about whether that accent was in fact a stress accent, like the one I was taught to misplace, or a pitch accent, like the Greek ones which confused Dorothea Brooke. Either way, I certainly wasn't getting a very good grounding in the language. When Robert Browning's Fra Lippo Lippi sings:

> Flower o' the clove
> All the Latin I construe is, 'amo' I love![12]

he at least knows enough Latin to know where the stress in 'amo' falls − but then he was Italian, and they still pronounce it like that.

However, the fact that memorizing and chanting verbs can lead to distorted pronounciation is not the only reason for suggesting a different approach, since an inevitable consequence of the idea that learning verbs means learning to parrot them is that most language students cling timidly to a very small number of tenses. And no wonder, considering the magnitude of the task. If, for instance, you wanted to learn a complete Italian verb off by heart, this would mean committing to memory, in the correct order, no fewer than forty-seven very similar words − and that's before you get to the compound tenses, and leaving out the participles and gerunds. Admittedly, Italian is a highly inflected language[13] so its verbs are quite complex. However, even Swedish verbs, which are six times as easy since there are no inflections within the tenses, are not exactly simple to learn off by heart. Here is the first conjugation Swedish verb *kalla*: to call (or rather: to call, name, designate, nominate, appoint, call in or send for, take the name of, feel fitted for). It is all in the first person singular, which is all you need to learn. Have a go.

ACTIVE VOICE. Present: jag kallar. Past: jag kallade. Future: jag ska kalla. Conditional: jag skulle kalla. Present perfect: jag har kallat. Past perfect: jag hade kallat. Future perfect: jag ska ha kallat. Conditional perfect: jag skulle ha kallat. Imperative: kalla! PASSIVE VOICE. Present: jag kallas. Past: jag kallades. Future: jag ska kallas. Conditional: jag skulle kallas. Present perfect: jag har kallats. Past perfect: jag hade kallats. Future perfect: jag ska ha kallats. Conditional perfect: jag skulle ha kallats.

Even when you have committed this to memory, along with a similar example from each of the other three conjugations, you will still have all the irregular verbs to reckon with. And of course you will have to be able to use your sample conjugations to work out the tenses of any other Swedish verbs you encounter, otherwise you will have learnt them in vain.

There has to be a better way of doing it, and fortunately there is. Even when learning the twelve times table, which you really do have to commit to memory (at any rate if you want to be able to do simple arithmetic without the help of a pocket calculator) it helps enormously if you notice the elegant and intriguing patterns which link the numbers together,[14] and pattern recognition is even more crucial in mastering verbs. However, while you only need to understand a single principle to make sense of the whole of the twelve times table, since the statement 'twice three is six' is mathematically no different from the statement 'seven times nine is sixty-three', the same thing does not hold true of the uses of, say, the present subjunctive and the past perfect tenses; so in the early stages of learning to live with verbs you will have to combine working at pattern recognition with taking on board quite a lot of grammatical information.

As with learning vocabulary, the easiest way of doing this is through patient close reading, since this ensures that you will be dealing with verbs encountered in meaningful contexts, not caged in the zoo of a grammar book. It is far easier to remember grammatical information which has helped you to solve a real-life language problem. This also means that you will not be meeting the various persons and tenses in any pre-arranged order, but that isn't a problem. Your previous language experience, whether it was a taped course for beginners or studying for a public exam, will mean that you have already met the tenses which any programmatic syllabus would begin with (even if you may not have realized what all of them were) so just tackle your verbs in the order in which they happen to appear on the page.

You will need the whole of your language tool-kit, since to start with you will have to find out three different things about every verb you meet: its person and tense, for which you will need your book of verbs; the job that particular tense does, for which you will need your reference grammar; and, last but not least, what the word on the page actually means, for which you will need your bilingual dictionary. You can see now why I suggested earlier that reading foreign-language books for children is quite a challenging task, but it will get easier once you have got your head round things like the difference between the perfect and the imperfect tense and worked out what subjunctives are for. However, even when you have put together all the information you need to make sense of your verb and the sentence you found it in, you still have one very important task. You need to look carefully at all the words that make up that particular tense of that particular verb, thinking as you do so about what each bit of it means. If you do this with enough tenses of enough verbs, you will begin to spot the patterns which enable native speakers to recognize the tenses and (if these are signalled by inflections rather than pronouns) the persons of regular verbs without needing to stop and think about it.

Which brings us to irregular verbs, the most eccentric and appealing of all parts of speech. The inventor of Esperanto, Dr L. L. Zamenhof, regarded it as a selling point that his synthetic language contained no irregular verbs, and indeed it hardly could have done unless they had been created by a linguistic version of the kind of 'distressing' which gives mock antique furniture its heritage look. Irregular verbs became irregular for the same reason that the treads of spiral staircases in old monasteries gradually became scooped and worn as the centuries went by. Like the bare feet of the monks slowly wearing away the hard stone, so the tongues and palates of generations of speakers wore down the commonest and most frequently used verbs into irregular shapes which would sit more comfortably in the mouth. So treasure your irregular verbs; a language without them is a language without a past.

Fortunately, they really aren't much harder to get used to than regular verbs, since you will be meeting the most important ones so often. You set about learning them in much the same way, though here you are looking out for several different kinds of pattern. There are the patterns which enable you to recognize that particular verb and to find your way about in it, the patterns which remind you of the regular verb it may once have been, or that have survived partly unchanged, and the patterns which often link groups of irregular verbs together, since they have been worn down into similar comfortable shapes. The most important irregular verbs to get on friendly terms with are the ones used as auxiliary verbs (the verbs which enable us to say things like 'I *am* feeling ill' and 'I *have* seen the doctor'). In the sample Swedish verb we looked at earlier, a lot of the work was being done by the auxiliary verbs *vara*: to be (with its irregular future and conditional tenses *ska* and *skulle*) and *hava*: to have; and since they do exactly the same job for all Swedish verbs, getting to know them is half the battle.

It goes without saying that you will probably have to adapt at least some of the above advice to suit the idiosyncrasies of the verbs in the particular language you are learning. Language is impossible without verbs, but that doesn't mean that their forms are universal. In fact, they have evolved in many different ways to suit the needs of different cultures. Swedish verbs have no subjunctives (the tenses used for talking about things which are not facts but suppositions, beliefs, doubts, fears, dreams and imaginings) but they are an important feature of Italian verbs. Classical Greek verbs had a middle voice as well as an active and a passive one, so that as well as talking about what the subject of the verb did or had done to it they could also talk about what it did to or for itself – leading to such ingenious idiomatic usages as 'I carry off for myself' (i.e. I win a prize) and 'I persuade myself' (i.e. I trust or believe in someone or something). Japanese verbs make do with just two tenses, the present and the past, but make up for it with an elaborate inbuilt code to do with politeness and relative social status. Just be glad that you have no need to learn the most difficult verbs of all: English phrasal verbs, from which, as Samuel Johnson said in the *Preface* to his *English Dictionary*, 'arises to foreigners the greatest difficulty'. His account vividly expresses the problem, even if some of his examples have been replaced by more recent but no less confusing ones:

> We modify the signification of many verbs by a particle subjoined; as to *come off*, to escape by a fetch; to *fall on*, to attack; to *fall off*, to apostatize; to *break off*, to stop abruptly; to *bear out*, to justify; to *fall in*, to comply; to *give over*, to cease; to *set off*, to embellish; to *set in*, to begin a continual tenour; to *set out*, to begin a course or journey; to *take off*, to copy; with innumerable expressions of the same kind, of which some appear wildly irregular, being so far distant from the sense of the simple words, that no sagacity will be able to trace the steps by which they arrived at the present one.[15]

For anyone who managed at an early age to master a language like that, no later feats of language learning are impossible.

The translator's craft

non verbum e verbo, sed sensum exprimere de sensu

translate not word for word but sense for sense

St Jerome

In 1768, the Presbyterian minister and classical scholar Edward Harwood published a *Liberal Translation of the New Testament*, claiming on the title page, with modest pride, that it was 'An Attempt to translate the Sacred Writings with the same Freedom, Spirit, and Elegance, with which other English Translations from the Greek Classics have lately been executed'. Further down the page he set out the excellent principles on which he had based his work:

> The Design and Scope of each Author being strictly and impartially explored, the True Signification and Force of the Original critically observed, and, as much as possible, transfused into our Language, and the Whole elucidated and explained upon a new and rational plan.

Combining scholarly attention to the original with a concern for the style of his English version, Harwood appeared to be set fair to achieve that fusion of textual analysis with creative writing in which the translator's art consists. Sadly, however, the result of his attempt to replace the 'bald and barbarous language' of the King James Version with something more fitting and up-to-date was that this:

> When I was a child, I spake as a child, I understood as a child, I thought as a child: but when I became a man, I put away childish things.
>   For now we see through a glass, darkly; but then face to face: now I know in part; but then shall I know even as also I am known.

became converted into this:

> Just as when I was, for example, in the imperfect state of childhood; I then discoursed, I understood, I reasoned in the erroneous manner children do – but when I arrived at the maturity

and perfection of manhood, the defects of my former imperfect
state were all swallowed up and forgotten.

For in this scene of being our terrestrial mirrour exhibits to us
but a very dim and obscure reflection: but in an happy futurity
we shall see face to face – In the present life my knowledge is
partial and limited: in the future, my knowledge will be
unconfined and clear, like that divine infallible knowledge, by
which I am now pervaded.

Dennis Freeborn, who includes Harwood's rendition of Chapter 13 of St Paul's Letter to the Corinthians in his *From Old English to Standard English*,[16] rightly remarks that 'present-day readers
are . . . likely to find [this] so overblown as to read like a parody'.[17]
Translators, however scrupulous, cannot help reflecting the spirit of
their age, but, given that Harwood published his *Liberal Translation* in
the decade that also saw the publication of Laurence Sterne's *Tristram
Shandy*, a work of fiction so inventive that it was not equalled until
James Joyce wrote *Ulysses*, it can hardly be claimed that this was a
period in which lively, forceful writing was a rarity. Harwood failed
in his grandiose attempt, not because he lived in the eighteenth
century but because, despite his protestations, he lacked both the
humility to attend to the 'true significations' of the original and the
musical ear for tone and register which would have allowed him to
transmit those meanings to his English readers. The entry on Harwood
in the *Dictionary of National Biography* drives home the point that it is
not enough for a translator to take care of the sense while leaving the
sounds to take care of themselves:

His 'liberal' rendering of the New Testament . . . was an honest
attempt . . . But Harwood's style was turgid; hence his translation has been visited with a contempt which on the grounds of
scholarship it ill deserves.

As this salutary example suggests, the translator's art can be learnt
only through years of disciplined attentiveness to the nuances of
language, though, unlike the art of the novelist, poet or dramatist,
which it otherwise resembles, it depends on pulling off a technically
impossible feat (no translation can really match the original) while
making that feat invisible to the audience (a translation should
create the illusion that nothing separates the reader from the
original). It goes without saying that, like all arts, it can be learnt

but it cannot be taught, though everything that you translate with serious thought and care will bring you a little closer to achieving it. The translator's craft is quite another matter. This too requires practice and perseverance, but at least it is not difficult to explain how to set about it.

As with any craft, you need to begin with the right tools for the job, which in your case means a bilingual dictionary, a reference grammar and a table of regular and irregular verbs. Monolingual dictionaries (both of the language you are translating from and of the language you are translating into) can also be useful, as can a thesaurus. You need to use a bilingual dictionary that will give you access not just to as large a vocabulary but also to as large a stock of idioms as possible, so try looking up the entries for some common words (such as the verbs 'to do', 'to make' and 'to go') to check how substantial and detailed they are.

In addition to your tool-kit of reference books, you may also want to use the published work of previous translators. However, there are two different dangers to beware of here. Firstly, the translation you consult may not be accurate. Many professional translators are so poorly paid that they are forced to produce speedy, and therefore shoddy, work, with the inevitable result that published translations are often riddled with errors. Secondly, a translation, like any other piece of writing, is the intellectual property of its author and any unacknowledged use of it is plagiarism. Otherwise honest and careful people sometimes make the mistake of thinking that translations, like the answers at the back of the school maths book, can be copied guiltlessly and undetected. In fact there are as many different and recognizable translations of any text as there are translators of it. You need to make quite sure, when preparing for a translation exam, that you do not get the wording of one particular translation so firmly pinned into your head that you reproduce it in your exam script. This is one area where it really is all too possible to commit plagiarism by accident.

Having assembled your tool-kit, your first task as a translator is to go through the passage to be translated with the same kind of explicatory attention that you would give to a difficult poem in English, thinking long and hard not just about the possible meanings of individual words and phrases but about what the author is actually trying to say. If you find it helpful to scribble suggestions on the text itself, make a xerox copy and scribble on that. You will need a clean copy of the text later on.

Your second task is to make a literal translation of the passage with the help of your dictionary, reference grammar and verb table. Don't bother about prose style at this stage, or even about English word order, and list possible variants of words or phrases rather than choosing between them.

The third stage is to put away the passage, shut your reference books, and concentrate on turning your literal translation into good, clear, natural English prose (or even verse). Remember that what you are trying to convey is the meaning of the passage, not its word order, and beware of those tell-tale awkwardnesses of expression which are the mark of translatorese. If any part of your translation looks like nonsense, you must have got something wrong; look up the vocabulary again (remembering that there will be a choice of more capacious dictionaries in the reference section of your university library) and, if that doesn't work, try some intelligent lateral thinking. In the last resort, a sensible guess may well be correct and will certainly be preferable to gibberish.

The final stage is to go back to the original passage and carefully check both that you have not left out any words or phrases and that you have not mistaken or misrepresented anything when making your idiomatic English version. (You need a clean copy of the text to do the latter, as otherwise you could easily be misled by your own marginalia.)

A couple of important points to bear in mind are firstly that it is part of your task as a translator to track down the significance of any references in the text you are translating: if your author alludes to the Biblical injunction to be 'wise as serpents',[18] it is no use translating it as 'clever as snakes'. Secondly, you need to think hard about proper names. Are Giuseppe, Maria and their little boy Gesù a family of devout Calabrian peasants, in which case their names need to stay in Italian, or are they the holy family, who need to be translated as Joseph, Mary and Jesus?

Finally, you need to remember that languages do not map perfectly on to each other, and inevitably there are some problems for which there is no good solution. Mozart wrote a charming early opera called *La Finta Giardiniera*: its title, snappy and effective in Italian, means 'the fake or feigned female gardener'. When Opera North put on a production a few years ago with the libretto brilliantly translated by Amanda Holden, both she and they finally admitted defeat over the title and left it in the original. Sometimes an explanatory footnote is the best you can do with a conundrum like this; sometimes a bold deviation from the literal meaning will get you round the problem, but that too will require an explanatory footnote.

Preparing for translation exams

Of course, you may be writing your translation in a closed exam, and in that case you will need a different technique. Here everything depends on how carefully you prepare the set material from which the short exam passages will be chosen. The way to do this is as follows:

1: Language learning is like learning to play a musical instrument: half an hour's practice every day is worth far more than a whole evening's practice once a week. Aim to do some preparation on most, if not all, of the available days.

2: Work out how many available days you have actually got, subtract two or three for consolidation at the end, and divide up the passages to be prepared into as many short chunks as you have days to prepare them in.

3: On day one, go through the first of your short chunks using your translator's tool-kit and work out what everything means. If you want to scribble on the text, make a xerox copy and scribble on that. It is essential to use an unmarked copy of the text: there will be no comforting annotations in the exam room.

4: On day two, read through yesterday's chunk in your unmarked copy of the text. You will have forgotten some of the vocabulary, so look it up again. Then prepare the second chunk.

5: On day three, read through the previous two chunks in your unmarked copy of the text. You will have forgotten some of the vocabulary, especially of chunk number two, so look it up again. Then prepare the third chunk.

6: By day four, the first chunk will be starting to look like an old friend. Keep on repeating the process and the whole of the set material will become equally familiar. When you get into the exam room, you won't need to waste time puzzling over what the passages mean, and if you have forgotten the odd word or two it will be easy to make intelligent guesses.

Chapter 10

Referencing

Due acknowedgement

When researching your essay, you will often have occasion to consult the work of other scholars and critics. The extent to which you do so will obviously depend upon the subject and your way of approaching it; what is important is that, whenever your written work makes use of the work of others, your indebtedness must be fully acknowledged. Direct quotations should be in quotation marks or indented, and attributed in such a way as to make it easy for the reader to look up their sources. If you paraphrase or summarize the work of another writer (or, indeed, lecturer) or adopt his or her conclusions, you should indicate clearly whose work you are using, where you begin to do so, and where you resume your own argument.

Simply putting the work in question in your bibliography is nothing like sufficient; instead you must footnote or end-note each specific instance of indebtedness. You should also make sure that you include in the essay itself the name of any writer whose ideas you quote or paraphrase, plus the title of the relevant publication:

> as Roy Porter says in *Enlightenment: Britain and the Creation of the Modern World* . . .

The same duty of acknowledgement also applies to the quotation of quotations. If you quote a passage from a book you have not read, you need to acknowledge not only the original source of that passage but also the fact that it was quoted by the author in whose pages you found it.

Such acknowledgement is a principle of academic courtesy, due both to the author whose work is used and to the reader. Plagiarism, the deliberate use of another's work as one's own, is the unforgivable academic sin and proclaims the culprit no scholar, so even the appearance of it must be scrupulously avoided. It therefore goes without saying that if, when researching your essay, you copy into your own notes a passage from any book (even one you don't expect to quote from) you should make sure that those notes include full bibliographical details of the book in question plus the relevant page number or numbers. Not only does this safeguard you against the accidental theft of other people's intellectual property, it also saves you from the maddening task of checking up later on information you ought to have jotted down at the time.

In an examination context, plagiarism is not only a sin but a serious crime, with potentially draconian consequences for the detected culprit. Conscientious students sometimes get very worked up at the possibility that they may commit plagiarism by accident, but there really is no danger of this provided you scrupulously follow all the above advice. Happening to invent a turn of phrase which some other writer, unbeknown to you, has already thought of is not plagiarism and would never be treated as such. Composing an entire paragraph which accidentally duplicates the work of a distinguished critic to whose book you could have had access is – despite what people sometimes tell you about monkeys, typewriters and the Complete Works of Shakespeare – not something which could occur by chance.

Footnotes and bibliographies

The neatest way of giving references to the sources of material quoted in your essay is to number your quotations and either footnote them with appropriate references or add a correspondingly numbered list of notes to the end of the essay. It looks neater if the number of the footnote or end-note follows any punctuation marks at the end of the quotation. Putting the reference itself in parentheses after the quotation is distracting and to be avoided. Apart from page numbers, your footnotes or end-notes need only contain enough information to enable your reader to find the relevant works in your bibliography – something which can be quite important if footnotes are included in the word limit of exam essays. Just stick to the following rules, which also apply to material you refer to or paraphrase. (Incidentally, the reason I have used a different convention for the notes in this book is because it causes the reader more inconvenience to have to search for bibliographical details at the back of a book than at the end of an essay.)

1: If you quote from just one work by one author called Warner, then 'Warner, p. 113' is all you need.

2: If you quote from more than one work by, or more than one author called, Woolf, then you will need to add a title keyword and/ or an initial: V. Woolf, *Lighthouse*, pp. 199–200; V. Woolf, *Moments*, pp. 64–5; L. Woolf, pp. 177–8.

3: If you quote from a work in more than one volume, then you will need to give both volume and page numbers: V. Woolf, *Diary*, vol. III, p. 208.

4: If you quote from a book which exists in a number of editions with different pagination, it will help your reader to locate the passage if you give chapter as well as page references: Austen, ch. 23, p. 238.

5: If you quote from a chapter by one author in a book of essays edited by another, you need only give the author's name plus page reference, as your bibliography will give all the other necessary details. However, if you quote from more than one work by that author, you should add title keywords to identify the book: Broughton, p. 123 *or* Broughton, *Women's Lives*, p. 123.

6: If you quote from a work that has been translated, you need give only the author's name in the end-note, but make sure you identify the translator in your bibliography: Proust, p. 357.

7: If you quote from a poem without mentioning its title in your text, then a page number in the *Collected Poems* cited in your bibliography will not be a helpful way of identifying it. Give the title plus the relevant line numbers instead: Hardy, *During Wind and Rain*, lines 8–14.

8: If you quote from a long poem divided into sections (or books, cantos or fyttes) give the number of the relevant section, plus line numbers if your edition includes them: Yeats, *Nineteen Hundred and Nineteen*, I, lines 41–3; Wordsworth, Bk I, lines 586–94; Dante, *Purg.* 28, lines 49–51.

9: If you quote from a play, you should give the author's name and act and scene numbers, plus line numbers if your edition includes them. If the play is by Shakespeare, you can give the title, or title keyword(s), rather than his name: *Tempest*, Act I, sc. 2, lines 399–405.

10: If you quote from the Bible, you should give book, chapter and verse: Ecclesiastes, ch. 7, 1–4.

11: If you quote from a poem (or short story) in an anthology, you should give the anthologist's name as well as the poet's. (Incidentally if, as in this example, the author's name is unknown, you should credit the poem to Anon., short for Anonymous): Anon., *The Unquiet Grave*, De La Mare, pp. 341–2.

12: If you quote from an article in a journal, you need only give the author's name plus a page reference, unless you are also quoting from something else by the same author, since your bibliography will give the name of the journal: McCombe, pp. 279–80.

13: If you quote from a website, you need only give the author's surname (plus the filename if you are quoting from more than one file on the same site) as your bibliography will give all the other necessary details: Ingram *or* Ingram, 'Family History'.

14: If you paraphrase or refer to material from a lecture, you need to give the lecturer's surname and the date of the lecture: Finkelbaum, lecture 29 February 2003. You also need to give full details of the lecture at the start of your bibliography.

15: If you quote from the same work twice or more running, you can replace the author's name (plus initial and/or title key-word) with *ibid*. (short for *ibidem*, which is Latin for 'in the same place').

16: If you quote from a work you quoted earlier in the essay, you can replace the author's name etc with *op. cit.* (short for *opere citato*, which is Latin for 'the work already quoted from') provided the identity of the text in question is clear from the context.

Putting it all together, the end-notes should look something like this:

References

1 Warner, p. 113.
2 V. Woolf, *Lighthouse*, pp. 199–200.
3 V. Woolf, *Diary*, vol. III, p. 208.
4 Austen, ch. 23, p. 238.
5 Broughton, p. 123.
6 Proust, p. 357.
7 Hardy, *During Wind and Rain*, lines 8–14.
8 Yeats, *Nineteen Hundred and Nineteen*, I, lines 49–51.
9 *Tempest*, Act I sc 2, lines 399–405.
10 Ecclestiastes, ch. 7, 1–4.
11 Anon., *The Unquiet Grave*, De La Mare, pp. 341–2.
12 McCombe, pp. 279–80.
13 Ingram, 'Family History'.
14 Finkelbaum, lecture 29 February 2003.
15 V. Woolf, *Moments*, pp. 64–5.
16 *Ibid.*, p. 40.
17 *Ibid.*, p. 78.
18 L. Woolf, pp. 177–8.
19 Dante, *Purg.* 28, lines 49–51.
20 Wordsworth, Bk I, lines 586–94.
21 *Op. cit.*, p. 107.

Footnotes or end-notes can also contain interesting ideas or relevant information which you have been unable to include in the essay itself. Remember that looking up notes will cause the reader a certain amount of extra trouble, so don't add them unnecessarily in the hope that they will make your essay appear more scholarly. Common sense suggests that notes of this sort may easily get overlooked among a long list of page numbers, so it is a good idea to put any fascinating additional nuggets of information in footnotes (indicated by asterisks or roman numerals) while tucking references away in end-notes.

At the end of your essay, you should list all the works used in preparing it in a detailed bibliography. (This is a far less daunting task if you compile the bibliography item by item while you are actually writing the essay itself.) There is more than one way of setting out a bibliography but, whichever conventions you adopt, you should make sure that you include all of the following information about books and journal articles:

> Author's Name, 'Title of Part of Book', *Title of Book*, ed. Editor's Name / trans. Translator's Name (Place of Publication and/or Publisher, Date)

> Author's Name, 'Title of Article', *Name of Journal*, Vol and No of issue, Date

If you want to cite material you have found on the Web, your reference should include the following information:

> Author's Name / Login Name / Alias (if any), 'Title of file', *Title of Website*, version/file number/date (if any), protocol full URL (Date of access)

NB: 'protocol' means the bit before www in a Web address (e.g. http://) and 'URL' (which stands for Universal Resource Locator) means the rest of the address – make sure that all the dots are in the right places and don't insert any spaces.

Your bibliography should be arranged in alphabetical order of authors' surnames (yes, I know it seems obvious, but it may not be to some) with multiple texts by a single author arranged consistently either alphabetically or chronologically (by date of first publication, not by the dates of the editions you happened to use). Any information you are unable to include in the bibliography proper can go in a prefatory note.

While you don't have to stick exactly to my suggested layout, there are one or two variations which are positively unhelpful to the reader. There is a recent fashion for making the referencing of books and articles in humanities subjects conform to the conventions for scientific ones by giving the publication date immediately after the author's name in bibliographies, and using dates rather than keywords in footnotes and end-notes. This makes perfect sense if you are a biochemist or particle physicist. Since the experimental data in Bunsen and Quark's latest paper supersedes that in their previous one, the reader needs to known that it is Bunsen and Quark, 2004F that is being cited rather than Bunsen and Quark, 2004E (let alone 2004D, C or B). In the case of Jane Austen, however, the publication date of the paperback copy of *Emma* you happened to buy contains no information about the vintage of the novel and should logically be attached to the name of the publisher. And while 'Jane Austen, 2003, *Emma* (Penguin)' merely looks anachronistic, 'Austen,

2003' in a footnote forces the reader to consult the bibliography to find out what you are quoting from, only to discover, as like as not, that your copies of *Northanger Abbey* and *Sense and Sensibility* were also published in 2003.

And, on a purely typographical note, bullet-pointing or numbering all the items in your bibliography, or preceding each one with a dash, makes it surprisingly hard to scan down the list of authors' names to locate particular items. It is far better to indicate where a new item starts by leaving a line space after the previous one, or by indenting the second and subsequent lines of each item. (You can set this indenting automatically in Word.)

Finally, here is the bibliography for 'Sea Change and Siren Voices: Childhood and Loss in Virginia Woolf's *To the Lighthouse*', the essay which generated the above set of end-notes. Although this is an imaginary essay by a fictitious student (let's call her Elinor Dashwood), the references are real. You will see that Elinor has used not just Woolf's own autobiographical writings, plus some critical and biographical essays, but a whole range of other relevant material, including Wordsworth's great poem about childhood and the growth of the imagination; Yeats's reflections on transience; a traditional ballad about mourning unduly prolonged; Dante's evocation of the as yet untouched Proserpina, soon to lose and be lost to her mother (taking sensible advantage of a GCSE in Italian and a parallel text, Elinor has quoted the lines in Italian); and – prompted both by McCombe's article (you couldn't make *his* title up) and by the name of the journal it appears in – Ariel's song 'Full fathom five' from *The Tempest*, in which the bones of a drowned father are transformed 'into something rich and strange'.

I am including her bibliography in full, not just to show you how to set out your own but also to illustrate a point I made earlier: an imaginative sense of the possibilities open to you can transform your idea of what relevance means and free you from the 'bare island' and its solipsistic texts. Elinor's island, like Shakespeare's in *The Tempest*, is 'full of noises, / Sounds and sweet airs . . . and sometime voices'.[1] No ship wrecked mariner she, whatever mark she was awarded for her essay.[2]

Bibliography

Some of my ideas about Virginia Woolf's relationship with her parents were developed from Professor Eve Finkelbaum's inspiring lecture, *Same Difference: Notes Toward a Taxonomy of Gender* (Visiting Lecture, University of Skerryvore, 29 February 2003) though I have ventured to dissent from her reading of the concluding part of *To the Lighthouse*.

All quotations from Wordsworth's *Prelude* are taken from the 1805 version.

Primary Sources

Woolf, Virginia, *To the Lighthouse* (Hogarth Press, 1977)

Woolf, Virginia, *Moments of Being: Unpublished Autobiographical Writings*, ed. Jeanne Schulkind (Sussex University Press, 1976)

The Diary of Virginia Woolf: Vol. III 1925–1930, ed. Anne Olivier Bell (Hogarth Press, 1980)

Secondary Sources

Austen, Jane, *Persuasion* (Penguin, 1965)

Holy Bible: Authorized King James Version

Broughton, Trev Lynn, 'Leslie Stephen, Anny Thackeray Ritchie, and the Sexual Politics of Genre: Missing Her', in *Women's Lives / Women's Times: New Essays on Auto/Biography*, ed. Trev Lynn Broughton and Linda Anderson (State University of New York Press, 1997)

Dante Alighieri, *The Divine Comedy of Dante Alighieri: Purgatory*, trans Robert M. Durling (Oxford University Press Inc., 2004)

De La Mare, Walter, *Come Hither, an Anthology of Poems* (Constable, 1967)

The Complete Poems of Thomas Hardy (Macmillan, 1976)

Ingram, Malcolm, 'Family History', *Virginia Woolf's Psychiatric History* (undated), http://ourworld.compuserve.com/homepages/famhist.htm

McCombe, John P., '"The Voyage Out": No "Tempest" in a Teapot: Woolf's Revision of Shakespeare and Critique of Female Education', *Ariel: A Review of International English Literature*, vol. 31, nos 1 & 2, Jan.–April 2000

Proust, Marcel, *The Guermantes Way*, in *Remembrance of Things Past*, vol. 2, trans. C. K. Scott Moncrieff and Terence Kilmartin (Penguin, 1989)

Shakespeare, William, *The Tempest*, ed. Frank Kermode (Arden Edition, Methuen, 1976)

The Diaries of Sylvia Townsend Warner, ed. Claire Harman (Virago Press, 1995)

Wordsworth, William, *The Prelude: A Parallel Text*, ed. J. C. Maxwell (Penguin, 1971)

Woolf, Leonard, *The Village in the Jungle* (Oxford University Press, 1981)

Yeats, W. B., *The Collected Poems* (Macmillan, 1950)

Chapter 11

Presentation

Studying your academic reader

Popular novelists (or novelists who would like to be popular) are often advised to study their readers. It is not always easy for the novelists to follow this advice since they may have no way of knowing whether they are most widely read by politicians, pensioners or plumbers. The writers of student essays do not have this problem; student essays are read by academics. It is worth giving a little thought to the academic reader as a species.

Academics have to do a great deal of reading in the course of their work. They read not only works of scholarship and imagination, not only student essays and exam scripts and dissertations and theses, but also minutes, reports, references, UCAS forms, letters from headteachers. Many of them have long ceased to enjoy the act of reading for its own sake. Many of them wear glasses. When academics do read student essays and exam scripts, they tend to do it late into the night and with the essays piled up in heaps. Being only human, they often sort through these heaps, which may contain as many as forty or fifty essays, and pick out the decently presented ones to read first. The most eye strain-inducing essay in the heap is therefore likely to be read last and late and when the reader is in a state of exhaustion.

The manufacturers of biscuits know that it is the look of the packet that sells the product. Academics are trained to be scrupulously fair in their judgements – it is unlikely that careful presentation of a mediocre essay will fool them into awarding it extra marks – but it is surprising how even the most appetizing ideas can lose their appeal if the taster is barely able to extract them from the packet.

All about layout

It is a too little known fact that it is possible to force a computer and its printer to conspire together in the production of text which is harder to read than the most illegible handwriting. It is done by breaking all the following simple rules.

1: The golden rule of good layout is summed up in the single word SPACE. The more blank space you leave on a page, the easier that page will be to read. The default settings of your word-processing package will ensure that you have an adequate margin on all four sides of the paper. Don't override them, however economical and tree-saving it may seem to dispense with margins altogether. Leave at least a triple line space between your title and your first paragraph. It is a good idea to indent the first line of each paragraph rather than leaving a double space between unindented paragraphs, both because you want your reader to feel that the essay resembles a book, not a business letter, and because you need to be able to indicate whether you have started a new paragraph after a free-standing quotation. Either double space or 1.5 space the text of the essay, and leave a line space between notes. You should leave a single space after punctuation marks within a sentence, and either a single or a double space between a full stop, question mark or exclamation mark and the first word of the following sentence. Double spaces between sentences look elegant and are an aid to legibility, which is why this is a professional typists' convention, but your word-processing programme may try to undo them (and if you write for publication your copy editor certainly will, since double spaces can cause eye-catching gaps on pages with an even right margin).

2: 12-point type is easier to read than 10-point, and a plain typeface such as Times New Roman is easier to read than a fancy one such as *Brush Script* or **Ashley**.

3: You can make free-standing quotations stand out from your own prose by single spacing the former and double or 1.5 spacing the latter. You should certainly indent them and leave a line space before and after them. Don't strain your reader's eyes by using a smaller typeface for quotations than for the rest of your essay, and never italicize quotations (no matter who tells you to do it), especially quotations in the body of your text, unless you are doing it to signal that they are in a foreign language. Since one use of italics is for emphasis, italicizing quotations makes them jump out of the page, creating an effect reminiscent of the epistolary style of Queen Victoria:

> The Queen *never* could consent to it, both for public and for private reasons, and the assumption of its being *too much* for a Prince Royal of Prussia to *come* over to marry *the Princess Royal of Great Britain in* England is too *absurd* to say the least . . . Whatever may be the usual practice of Prussian Princes, it is not *every* day that one marries the eldest daughter of the Queen of England.[1]

4: Print your essay on plain white paper of decent thickness. Coloured paper (even beige or parchment) will make your essay harder to read and may even be a migraine trigger for some readers. Don't print on both sides of the paper unless it is satisfactorily opaque.

5: It is hard to read a page full of black and white streaks, and impossible for anyone to read an essay you can't print out. Make sure you always have a spare ink cartridge, especially if you are going to be handing in exam essays close to the deadline.

6: Remember to spell check your work carefully. Spell checking is a tedious and labour-intensive chore but worth it to sieve out at least some of the inevitable slips and typos.

7: Your finished essay will almost certainly contain some errors, even after it has been spell checked, so you will also need to proof-read it carefully before handing it in.

Proof-reading

Conscientious writers read through their completed work in no fewer than three different ways, and proof-reading – which means checking for typos, missing or misplaced punctuation marks, errors in layout and other technical glitches – is actually the last of the three. Firstly, you should read through your essay as objectively as possible, looking for any gaps in the argument or infelicities in the phrasing which need fixing. Secondly, you should check that all quotations are accurately attributed and your bibliography is complete. You may not have time to check the wording of every single quotation, but you should certainly look up any which appear to have been mistranscribed. Finally, you should go through your essay with the proverbial fine-tooth comb, looking for bugs. Professional proof-readers increase their efficiency by scanning the text carefully bit by bit rather than actually reading it, since readers tend to see what ought to be there rather than what actually is. This is even more important if you are proof-reading your own copy, since over-familiarity with the contents can make mistakes surprisingly hard to spot. Be especially vigilant in checking the title and the opening page, where a certainty that you must have got this bit right can cause the eye to glide over quite major errors. A colleague of mine once spent several hundred pounds on a massive two-volume seventeenth-century work called *The Monuments of the Kings of England*. At least, that is what Volume One was called. The title page of Volume Two, in 72-point type, bore the memorable inscription:

THE MONUMENTS OF THE KNIGS OF ENGLAND.

Safety in cyberspace

Safety in cyberspace comes under two headings, safeguarding your work and safeguarding your health. To prevent your essay from suddenly vanishing into a digital black hole, get into the habit of saving your work every ten minutes or so (you can pre-set most word-processing programs to do this automatically) and also back it up onto a floppy disk at the end of every computing session. For really important documents, such as exam essays, it is a good idea to keep two floppy disks and use them after alternate sessions. That way, if anything happens to one disk, you still have another containing most of your document.

Remember that with computers and their printers what can go wrong will, so make sure you print out your work well before the deadline to allow for unexpected failures of the system. For extra security, print out any important additions to the document at the end of each session. If total computer meltdown occurs, you can then do a low-tech scissors and paste job, neatly writing in the missing bits and xeroxing the end result; your essay will be legible and on time if slightly raffish-looking.

Safeguarding your health is a much more serious matter, since painful, and quite possibly irreversible, things can happen to people who neglect to take sensible precautions when using a computer.

Working with your monitor set up in a way which strains your neck, and failing to take adequate breaks, can lead to work-related upper limb disorders, the symptoms of which include temporary or chronic pain, swollen soft tissue, loss of movement in your joints, and – in the worst cases – permanent and crippling loss of function in your shoulders, arms, wrists and hands. Repetitive strain injury is no myth and is far too common, and believe me, it isn't any fun to live with.

To avoid all this, make sure that your monitor is at the correct height – the top of the screen should be set at eye level, so that you are not craning your neck to peer up at it – and take a five or ten minute break every fifty or sixty minutes. Short, frequent breaks will do you far more good than one substantial break after several hours' work, since the aim is to prevent the onset of fatigue, not to enable yourself to recover from it. Get up from your desk, stretch and walk about for a few minutes, preferably out of sight of your computer. This is especially important if you are working flat out on an essay and need to use your computer for long periods of the day (or, indeed, the night). Taking adequate breaks also allows your ideas to coalesce, so don't think of this as time lost, even if you are working to a tight deadline.

Apart from checking your monitor height, you can improve your workspace by using a comfortably supportive desk chair, adjusted for height so that your forearms are horizontal to the work surface. You may find that a mousemat with a built-in wrist support helps to prevent muscular fatigue, and, since the sideways movements of the forearm necessitated by using a conventional mouse can put considerable strain on the wrist and shoulder, it is worth investing in a rollerball mouse if you find that you are suffering from even mild mousing discomfort. Mild computer health problems can be the warning that more serious ones are on the horizon.

Holding it all together

If you hand in your essay as a pile of loose pages, these are likely to get lost on your reader's desk. That desk is unlikely to be a tidy one, or one on which a single stray page is easy to find. If you hand in your essay as a pile of loose pages with all the top left-hand corners dog-eared over, exactly the same thing will happen. Your idiocy will be compounded if those pages are also unnumbered.

How, then, are you to fasten the pages together? A paper clip is quite satisfactory. Stapling the top left-hand corner is even more satisfactory, provided you have left sufficient margin. Stapling all down the left-hand side when you have left no margin at all, and then tying little bits of metal-tagged green string in double granny knots through half a dozen holes, is a way of condemning your reader to twenty minutes' laborious untying and unpicking. Knotting the pages loosely together with a single straggling piece of thread is also to be deplored.

When deciding how to fasten your essay together, ask yourself these simple questions. Will the end-product be easy to read? Are the fastenings likely to irritate, or indeed (as in the case of dress-making pins and bits of wire) lacerate the reader? Common sense should then suggest the solution.

Handwriting in closed exams

Finally, don't let yourself become so dependent on email, texting and word processing that you allow your handwriting to atrophy. Since, as William Cobbett observes, 'thoughts come much faster than we can put them upon paper',[2] handwriting speed is a significant factor in performance in closed exams, and there are other desperate circumstances (from sudden computer breakdown to being stranded on a desert island) when legible handwriting (for that emergency hand-crafted essay or hopeful message in a bottle) could mean the difference between life and death. The only way to keep your handwriting up to speed is to make sure that there are regular and frequent occasions when you use it. Try writing an old-fashioned letter to your grandparents every week – they will be touched by the gesture and you will get the credit as well as the practice. Keeping a hand-written journal (in order, like Oscar Wilde's Gwendolen, to make sure you 'always have something sensational to read on the train'[3]) and making tidy and organized research notes are also useful ways to practise writing fast and fluently.

Though people who regularly mark closed exams get a lot of practice in deciphering difficult handwriting, and no examiner is going to give you extra marks for calligraphy however beautiful your italic script, it is still worth remembering that it is easier to do justice to the merits of a sustained argument if the mind is not being distracted by the physical business of reading. If your course is partly assessed by closed exams, take a look at your handwriting and see if you can make it more legible. For instance, if your handwriting is much too small, you should take the trouble to write larger each time you write anything, even a shopping list, and habit will soon solve the problem. If your handwriting is much too large, it is likely also to be slower than need be, since your hand is having to travel further to produce it. In addition, if you write very large on the kind of ruled paper handed out in exam rooms, all the lines of writing will knit themselves into a continuous fabric very hard for the reader to unravel, though that particular problem can be solved by simply writing on alternate lines. Ruled paper also contributes to another kind of illegibility, the kind that you can achieve by writing not on the lines but halfway between them so that the lines become a headache-inducing distraction to the reader's eye.

However, by far the commonest kind of illegibility is caused not by the size or alignment of the writing (though these can be contributing factors) but by the actual formation of the letters. The important thing to realize here is that the malformation of just two or three letters out of the twenty-six is enough to make a script unreadable. To deal with this problem, you need to look analytically at your handwriting, possibly enlisting the help of candid friends, in order to identify the baffling letters in your particular case. You will probably discover that the problem is quite a small-scale one when tackled in this way. If the funny way you write your *r* is identical to the funny way you write your *s*, this may be enough in itself to confuse your readers, but equally it is quite a simple job to relearn how to write those two letters. In order to achieve this, you may have to abandon the convention of completely joined-up writing and make a little break before or after your *r* or *s*. You may also have to abandon some treasured system of decorative scrolls and flourishes. These are small sacrifices if legibility results from them.

One of the simplest of such adjustments of individual letters is to learn to put the dot on the i, or in some cases to put the dot directly above the i instead of half a league onward. Similarly, crossing the *t* where the *t* actually is can make a world of difference for your readers. Whatever the changes needed in your particular case, you must, of course, take pains to use the improved versions of those letters in everything you write so that they quickly become second nature to you. Finally, if you are going to be sitting closed exams, don't try to transform your handwriting in any way that slows it down, and make sure you give yourself plenty of time to get up to speed with any changes before you actually find yourself in the exam room.

Chapter 12

Will-power

The commonest, and at times the most disabling, problem to afflict the student essay-writer has nothing to do with the niceties of prose style or the use of the apostrophe. It is the problem of actually getting the words down on paper. You may find it comforting to reflect that this is not simply a student problem but one that faces all writers everywhere, including great ones. In your case, however, the problem is made both simpler and more urgent by the fact that student essays have to be written to deadlines. This means that you cannot afford to write like James Joyce, squeezing out *Finnegans Wake* a page at a time; still less can you afford to write like Coleridge, who had the grandest ambitions but seldom managed to get down to it at all. Instead you must model yourself on Dickens or the young Kipling (or, indeed, despite the impression given by Stoppard's comic screenplay, Shakespeare) and adopt, as they had to, the professional attitude that meeting deadlines efficiently is an essential part of the job.

The thing which is most likely to prevent you from meeting deadlines efficiently is the cultivation in yourself of a case of false writer's block. Real writer's block is a very rare condition, affecting perhaps one student in a thousand. The patient, with no matter what exercise of will-power, is simply unable to put words of an academic kind down on paper. This condition, which can cause great distress to the sufferer, is in fact a symptom, not an ailment in itself. It can be caused by problems ranging from a mistaken choice of university course to medical or family troubles, and the cure for it is to tackle the causal problem directly. False writer's block is another matter entirely, and all too common.

The patient begins by feeling reluctant to write an essay. This reluctance, which really stems from that mixture of perfectionism and sloth which could be described as human nature, is instead attributed by the patient to writer's block (much as sufferers from the common cold dignify their ailment by telling themselves they have flu). Sympathetic attention from a tutor appears to confirm the diagnosis, and the patient finds the next essay even harder to write. If you have allowed yourself to get into this condition it can be quite hard to get yourself out of it again, but some of the following ideas may help.

All solid bodies have a property which scientists call inertia. This means that when things are stationary they want to remain station- ary, and when they are moving they want to continue to move. It follows that it takes far more effort to start something moving, when its inertia is acting against you, than it does to keep it moving, when its inertia is on your side. Inertia affects the essay-writer in two different ways. It is harder to write the opening paragraph than it is to write the rest of the essay, and it is harder to make yourself sit down at your desk than it is to keep on sitting there.

The difficulty of writing the opening paragraph can sometimes be overcome by pretending that the essay is a letter. You choose a sympathetic correspondent, write at the top of the page, 'Dear Mum / Professor Finkelbaum / Judi Dench, I thought you might be interested in some ideas I have had about syntax and subterfuge in the late novels of Henry James', and then launch straight into the subject. When the essay is finished, you trim down the opening sentence to leave you with a suitable title (or add a new one if necessary).

The difficulty of making yourself sit down at your desk is sensibly lessened if you write as much of your essay as possible at a single sitting. Getting up for a short break means having to get started all over again, and for many reluctant writers that short break can last for the rest of the day. If you can arrange for a house-mate, or the person in the next study-bedroom, to bring you in some coffee an hour or so after you start writing, it helps to pin you to your chair. Make sure you do the same for them if they need it. Some people also find that writing to music helps. This works best if you turn the sound down really low, so that you have a virtually subliminal rhythm keeping you going without breaking your concentration. If you are composing your essay at the keyboard, you will need to take a five to ten minute break every hour to rest your eyes and wrists and stretch your back, but don't let this turn into an excuse to go off and start doing something else. Developing a seven minute exercise routine, whether it is yoga or just walking up and down the room, is a good way of fending off temptation.

Some people find that writing at night gives them a good stretch of time free from distractions, but you should only write late at night if you are sure your nervous system can stand it. Messing about all day and then desperately starting work after midnight when all you want to do is sleep is a sure way of reinforcing false writer's block. The healthy option, if you are really pressed for time and can summon up the discipline, is to rise at five, as professional writers always claim they do (and sometimes really have to). Take it from me, once you are actually up and awake there is nothing to do at 5 a.m. *but* work. You will need an alarm clock. And a good big mug of tea or coffee. (And, if you share a bedroom with them, an understanding room-mate or partner.)

The difficulty of getting started often expresses itself in what are known as displacement activities: the writer gets started on something else instead. This can be fatal, especially if the something else is reading a book. It is possible to read the whole of *A Suitable Boy*[1] while not getting on with writing an essay on *Mansfield Park*. However, this is a psychological mechanism which can sometimes be put into reverse, so that you start writing your essay in order not to get on with the washing up. A more subtle form of displacement activity is to spin out the researching of your essay to unnecessary lengths. Reading one more book about Jane Austen can also be a way of not getting on with writing an essay on *Mansfield Park*.

Finally, it is worth remembering that, though feeling miserable can stop you from working, working, when once you have got started, can often stop you from feeling miserable.

Notes

Chapter 1

1 William Cobbett, *A Grammar of the English Language*, ed. Robert Burchfield (Oxford University Press, 1984), p. 4.
2 *Ibid.*, p. 143.
3 The first of these is serious advice; the second is a handy rule of thumb as long as your name isn't Sheila; and as for the third, try it and see.
4 Ben Jonson, 'Timber: or Discoveries', in *The Complete Poems*, ed. George Parfitt (Penguin, 1996), p. 378.

Chapter 2

1 Bk VI, lines 205–9.
2 *Gardenage or The Plants of Ninhursaga* (Routledge and Kegan Paul, 1952), p. 92.
3 Dante Alighieri, *Inferno*, Canto I, lines 85–7.
4 *Ulysses* (Bodley Head, 1960), p. 133.
5 Bk I, Ode XI, line 8.
6 Lines 79–80.
7 Bk III, lines 61–4.
8 *To the Virgins, to make much of Time.*
9 *Johnson: Poetry and Prose*, ed. Mona Wilson (Rupert Hart-Davis, 1970), p. 848.
10 *ABC of Reading* (Faber, 1973), p. 61.
11 *Quarterly Review*, no. 1.
12 Act III, sc. 3.
13 Act II, sc. 3.
14 *Johnson: Poetry and Prose*, p. 609.
15 Act IV, sc. 2.
16 *Mrs Dalloway* (Penguin, 1964), p. 154.
17 *To the Lighthouse* (Penguin, 1964), pp. 50–1.
18 Lines 41–2.
19 *Op. cit.*, p. 139.
20 *Ibid.*, p. 229.
21 *The Windhover*, lines 13–14.

22 See Philip Ball, *Bright Earth: The Invention of Colour* (Viking, 2001) for a more detailed account.
23 *Op. cit.*, pp. 56–7.
24 *Ibid.*, p. 145.
25 *Ibid.*, pp. 146–7.
26 Bk VI, line 702.
27 Bk XI, lines 206–8.
28 *The Diary of Virginia Woolf*, vol. III, ed. Anne Olivier Bell (Hogarth Press, 1980), p. 135.
29 *Ibid.*, p. 208.
30 *Lycidas*, line 72.
31 *The Goshawk* (Penguin, 1963), p. 87.
32 Wordsworth, *The Tables Turned*, lines 26–8.
33 *L'Allegro*, lines 133–4.
34 'Defence of the Epilogue, Or, An Essay on the Dramatique Poetry of the last Age' in *The Conquest of Granada by the Spaniards*.
35 *Johnson: Poetry and Prose*, p. 491.
36 Facsimile of copy in the Birmingham Shakespeare Library (Cornmarket Press, 1969), p. 24.
37 See Donald Davie, 'The Auroras of Autumn', in *The Achievement of Wallace Stevens*, ed. Ashley Brown and Robert S. Haller (New York: Gordian Press, 1973), in which a very distinguished critic bases an otherwise ingenious essay on this particular misreading.
38 Noam Chomsky, *Syntactic Structures* (The Hague: Monton, 1957), ch. 2.
39 Line 771.
40 *Heart of Darkness* (Penguin, 1973), p. 85.
41 *Ibid.*, p. 106.

Chapter 3

1 *Vertue*, line 5.
2 John Romer, *Testament: The Bible and History* (Michael O'Mara Books, 1988), p. 322. See chapter 7 for a full account of the King James Bible and its precursors.
3 Penguin, 1985.
4 Lion Publishing plc, 1998.
5 Cover blurb, attributed to Diamond Comics.
6 Romer, p. 327.
7 Daniel, 3, 23. See Apocrypha, The Song of the Three Holy Children.
8 Collins, 1987.
9 Oxford World's Classics, 1986.
10 Penguin, 1955.
11 Trans. Frank Justus Miller, 1916.
12 Penguin, 1990, and Penguin, 1996, respectively.
13 Princeton, 1959.
14 *Fiabe italiane: raccolte dalla tradizione popolare durante gli ultimi anni e trascritte in lingua dai vari dialetti da Italo Calvino* (Turin: Einaudi, 1956), translated as *Italian Folktales: Selected and Retold by Italo Calvino*, trans. George Martin (Penguin, 1982).

15　*Kinder- und Hausmärchen* (*Children's and Household Tales*), generally known in English as Grimms' Fairy Tales.
16　*Histoires ou contes du temps passé, avec des moralités: Contes de ma mère l'Oye* (*Stories or Tales from Times Past, with Morals: Tales of Mother Goose*).
17　*Travels with Virginia Woolf*, ed. Jan Morris (Pimlico, 1997), p. 138.
18　*The Road to Xanadu: A Study in the Ways of the Imagination* (Picador, 1978), p. 207.
19　*Narrative and Dramatic Sources of Shakespeare* (Routledge, 1957–75).
20　Angela Martin, *Virginia Wolves*, Cath Tate Cards, PO Box 647, London SW2 4JX. (Yes, you really do need to acknowledge *everything* you quote, from criticism to cartoon captions.)
21　Letter to Sir Horace Mann, 28 January 1754.

Chapter 4

1　W. C. Sellar and R. J. Yeatman, *1066 and All That: A Memorable History of England*, intr. Frank Muir (Alan Sutton, 1993), p. 89.
2　If you really are numb and vague about Arabella Stuart, you can find out all about her by reading Sarah Gristwood's biography *Arbella: England's Lost Queen* (Bantam Press, 2003).
3　William Shakespeare, *The Tempest*, Epilogue.

Chapter 6

1　Michael Heyward, *The Ern Malley Affair* (Faber, 1993), p. 65.
2　*A Grammar of the English Language*, p. 141.
3　W. H. Auden, *The Dyer's Hand and Other Essays* (Faber, 1963), p. 8.
4　Richard Brinsley Sheridan, *The Rivals*, Act III, sc. 3.
5　Sir Ernest Gowers, *The Complete Plain Words*, revised Sidney Greenbaum and Janet Whitcut (Penguin, 1987).
6　John Milton, *Paradise Lost*, Bk VII, line 402.
7　Lewis Carroll, *Through the Looking Glass*, ch. 6.
8　See Terry Eagleton, *After Theory* (Allen Lane, 2003).
9　*Literary Theory: A Very Short Introduction* (Oxford University Press, 1997), pp. 1–2.
10　Randall Jarrell, 'The Age of Criticism', in *Poetry and the Age* (Faber, 1955), p. 83.
11　*Traduttore: traditore.*
12　As in Shakespeare's *Tempest*, Act V, sc. 1, rather than Aldous Huxley's novel.
13　Note to the author.
14　Ben Jonson, 'Timber: or Discoveries made upon men and matter', *The Complete Poems*, ed. George Parfitt (Penguin, 1996), p. 434.
15　Samuel Johnson, 'Preface to the English Dictionary' in *Johnson: Poetry and Prose*, ed. Mona Wilson (Rupert Hart-Davis, 1970), p. 320.
16　*Ibid.*, p. 319.
17　*Ibid.*, p. 321.
18　William Shakespeare, *The Passionate Pilgrim* XX, lines 23–4.
19　Robert Herrick, *To God*.

20 Emily Dickinson, Poem 311 in *The Complete Poems of Emily Dickinson*, ed. Thomas H. Johnson (Faber, 1970).
21 William Wordsworth, *Resolution and Independence*, lines 61–3.
22 *The Guardian*, 19 September 2000, p. 2.
23 *Alice's Adventures in Wonderland*, ch. 1.
24 See Edward W. Said, *Culture and Imperialism* (Chatto and Windus, 1993).
25 William Blake, *The Marriage of Heaven and Hell*.
26 Quoted by Ernest Gowers in *The Complete Plain Words*, pp. 166–7.
27 *Structures or Why Things Don't Fall Down* (Penguin, 1991), p. 55.

Chapter 7

1 Samuel Johnson, 'The Plays of William Shakespeare: Concluding Notes' in *Samuel Johnson: A Critical Edition of the Major Works*, ed. Donald Greene (Oxford, 1984), p. 462.

Chapter 8

1 For the complete list see James Pitman and John St John, *Alphabets and Reading* (Sir Isaac Pitman and Sons Ltd, 1969), p. 65.
2 G. H. Vallins, *Spelling*, revised by D. G. Scragg (André Deutsch, 1965).
3 Quoted in Vallins, p. 85.
4 Examples are gaol/jail; mediaeval/medieval; taboo/tabu. In the case of the name of a mythological monster with an eagle's head and wings and a lion's body, no fewer than three spellings are possible: griffin, griffon and gryphon. However, the various kinds of Eurasian vulture and terrier-like dog which share the same name can only be spelt griffon, while a griffin is also both a newcomer or novice and a hint, signal or racing tip.
5 One area where American English is standardized while British English allows for variation is in the spelling of verbs ending in 'ise' or 'ize'. There are a number of verbs which invariably end in 'ise' on both sides of the Atlantic – including advertise, advise, arise, comprise, despise, devise, disguise, exercise, improvise, revise, supervise and surprise. In other cases, British writers are at liberty to choose between realise and realize, recognise and recognize, and so on, while American writers are obliged to use the 'ize' form. It follows that British writers can opt for 'ise' in all cases (except size and prize in the sense of value) and thus never make a mistake, while American writers (or their spell checks) need to be able to distinguish between verbs which always end in 'ise' and verbs which always end in 'ize'.
6 John Webster, *The Duchess of Malfi*, quoted in Geoffrey Grigson, *The Cherry Tree* (Phoenix House, 1959), p. xii.
7 Margaret J. Snowling, *Dyslexia* (Blackwell, 2000), p. 201.
8 *Ibid.*, p. 208.
9 Ben Jonson, *The English Grammar (from the Works) 1640* (facsimile, Scolar Press, 1972), p. 83.
10 Interview carried out for *The Shul in Aldwark: A History of the York Synagogue, 1892–1976*, to be published by The Borthwick Institute, University of York.

11 Quoted by Ernest Gowers, *The Complete Plain Words*, revised by Sidney Greenbaum and Janet Whitcut (Penguin, 1987), p. 152.

12 *A Grammar of the English Language*, ed. Robert Burchfield (Oxford University Press, 1984), p. 59.

13 Dickinson, *Selected Letters*, ed. Thomas H. Johnson (Harvard University Press, 1986), p. 174.

14 See *An Introduction to English Grammar* (Longman, 1991), pp. 11–17 and 101–13.

15 *Grammar*, p. 5.

16 *Mind the Stop* (Penguin, 1976), p. 121.

17 Act II, sc. 2.

18 Rudyard Kipling, 'The Cat that Walked by Himself', *Just So Stories For Little Children* (Macmillan, 1971), p. 199.

19 *Ibid.*, p. 206.

20 *To the Lighthouse* (Penguin, 1964), p. 188.

21 *Ibid.*, p. 217.

22 *Ibid.*, p. 236.

23 *Complete Plain Words*, p. 167.

24 *To the Lighthouse*, p. 147.

25 *Ibid.*, p. 236.

26 *Complete Plain Words*, p. 170.

27 Dennis Freeborn, *A Course Book in English Grammar*, 2nd edition (Palgrave, 1995), pp. 115–16.

28 Nick Robinson, ITV Lunchtime News, 27 November 2003.

29 If you have ever wondered about its famous opening line, 'Scots, wha hae wi' Wallace bled' just means 'Scots, who have with Wallace bled'.

30 Casey Miller and Kate Swift, *Words and Women* (Gollancz, 1977), p. 131.

31 *Ibid.*, p. 130.

32 E. Nesbit, *Five Children and It* (first published T. Fisher Unwin, 1902).

33 Act III, sc. 2.

34 Cheratra Yaswen, in her interesting on-line article *Those who thee and thou: the second person singular pronoun after 1800*, http://www.chass.utoronto.ca/~cpercy/courses/6362Yaswen2.htm (2003), quotes her mother's cousin Don Badgley as saying 'Some Quakers still use the thee and thou especially around Philly in the octogenarian set.'

35 *Ibid.*

Chapter 9

1 *Middlemarch* (Penguin, 1985), p. 32.

2 *Ibid.*, pp. 88–9.

3 *Introduction to Attic Greek* (University of California Press, 1993), p. 16.

4 *The Mill on the Floss* (Penguin, 1985), p. 217.

5 *Mythologies* (Éditions du Seuil, 1957), pp. 201 and 203; *Mythologies: Selected and Translated from the French*, trans Annette Lavers (Vintage, 1993), pp. 115–16 and 118. The example Barthes uses, 'quia ego nominor leo' (because my name is lion) – from Aesop's fable about the lion who demanded 'the lion's share' – would have delighted Maggie Tulliver.

6 *Op. cit.*, pp. 220–1.
7 *Ibid.*, p. 221.
8 *Nicomachean Ethics*, Bk 2.
9 55–57 Great Marlbrough Street, London, W1F 7AY: you can buy books from them by mail order.
10 *Ulysses* (Bodley Head, 1966), p. 804.
11 See Penny Lewis, 'Be Happy', *New Scientist*, 27 December 2003 to 3 January 2004, pp. 62–3.
12 *Fra Lippo Lippi*, lines 110–11.
13 An inflected language is one in which words are modified, through vowel changes or the addition of prefixes or suffixes, to express changes in (grammatical) number, case, gender, tense, mood etc.
14 Such as the fact that if you add together the digits which make up each product in the nine times table, they will always add up to nine.
15 Samuel Johnson, 'Preface to the English Dictionary', in *Johnson: Poetry and Prose*, ed. Mona Wilson (Rupert Hart-Davis, 1970), p. 309.
16 *From Old English to Standard English: A Course Book in Language Variation Across Time* (Macmillan, 1998).
17 *Ibid.*, p. 393.
18 Matthew, ch. 10, v. 16.

Chapter 10

1 Act III, sc. 2, lines 133–6.
2 Actually it was 79, later put up to 85 by Evie Finkelbaum, who happened to be one of the external examiners.

Chapter 11

1 Quoted in Lytton Strachey, *Queen Victoria* (Chatto and Windus, 1921), p. 203.
2 *A Grammar of the English Language*, edited by Robert Burchfield (Oxford University Press, 1984), p. 142.
3 *The Importance of Being Earnest*, Act II.

Chapter 12

1 No, you don't want to know the author's name. You've got an essay to write.

Bibliography

Auden, W. H. *The Dyer's Hand and Other Essays* (Faber, 1963)

Bacon, Francis, *Essays*, ed. Michael J. Hawkins (J. M. Dent and Sons, 1972)

Ball, Philip, *Bright Earth: The Invention of Colour* (Viking, 2001)

Barthes, Roland, *Mythologies* (Éditions du Seuil, 1957). *Mythologies: Selected and Translated from the French*, trans Annette Lavers (Vintage, 1993)

Beite, Ann-Mari, *Basic Swedish Grammar* (The Institute for English-Speaking Students, University of Stockholm, 1963)

Burchfield, R. W. *The New Fowler's Modern English Usage*, revised 3rd edition (Oxford University Press, 1998)

Carey, G. V. *Mind the Stop: A Brief Guide to Punctuation* (Penguin, 1976)

Chomsky, Noam, *Syntactic Structures* (The Hague: Monton, 1957)

Clare, John, *The Letters of John Clare*, ed. J. W. and Anne Tibble (Routledge and Kegan Paul, 1951)

Cobbett, William, *A Grammar of the English Language*, ed. Robert Burchfield (Oxford University Press, 1984)

Cuddon, J. A. *The Penguin Dictionary of Literary Terms and Literary Theory*, 4th edition (Penguin, 1999)

Culler, Jonathan, *Literary Theory: A Very Short Introduction* (Oxford University Press, 1997)

Dickinson, Emily, *Selected Letters*, ed. Thomas H. Johnson (the Belknap Press of Harvard University Press, 1986)

Eagleton, Terry, *After Theory* (Allen Lane, 2003)

Eagleton, Terry, *Literary Theory: An Introduction* (Blackwell, 1983)

Eco, Umberto, *Come si fa una tesi di laurea* (Milan: Bompiani, 1977)

Fox, George, *The Journal of George Fox*, ed. John L. Nickalls (Cambridge University Press, 1952)

Freeborn, Dennis, *A Course Book in English Grammar*, 2nd edition (Palgrave, 1995)

Freeborn, Dennis, *From Old English to Standard English: A Course Book in Language Variation Across Time*, 2nd edition (Macmillan, 1998)

Gordon, J. E. *Structures or Why Things Don't Fall Down* (Penguin, 1991)

Gowers, Ernest, *The Complete Plain Words*, revised by Sidney Greenbaum and Janet Whitcut (Penguin, 1987)

Greenbaum, Sidney, *An Introduction to English Grammar* (Longman, 1991)

Grigson, Geoffrey, *Gardenage or The Plants of Ninhursaga* (Routledge and Kegan Paul, 1952)

Gristwood, Sarah, *Arbella: England's Lost Queen* (Bantam Press, 2003)

Heyward, Michael, *The Ern Malley Affair* (Faber, 1993)

Jarrell, Randall, *Poetry and the Age* (Faber, 1955)

Johnson, Samuel, *Johnson: Poetry and Prose*, ed. Mona Wilson (Rupert Hart-Davis, 1970)

Johnson, Samuel, *Samuel Johnson: A Critical Edition of the Major Works*, ed. Donald Greene (Oxford University Press, 1984)

Jonson, Ben, 'Timber: or Discoveries', in *The Complete Poems*, ed. George Parfitt (Penguin, 1996)

Jonson, Ben, *The English Grammar (From the Works) 1640* (facsimile, Scolar Press, 1972)

Lodge, David, *Working with Structuralism* (Routledge and Kegan Paul, 1981)

Lowes, John Livingston, *The Road to Xanadu: A Story of the Ways of the Imagination* (Picador, 1978)

Mastronarde, Donald J. *Introduction to Attic Greek* (University of California Press, 1993)

Miller, Casey and Swift, Kate, *Words and Women* (Gollancz, 1977)

Pitman, James, and John St John, *Alphabets and Reading: The Initial Teaching Alphabet* (London: Sir Isaac Pitman and Sons Ltd, 1969)

Pound, Ezra, *ABC of Reading* (Faber, 1973)

Radice, William, and Barbara Reynolds, ed. *The Translator's Art: Essays in Honour of Betty Radice* (Penguin, 1987)

Romer, John, *Testament: The Bible and History* (Michael O'Mara Books, 1988)

Sellar, W. C. and R. J. Yeatman, *1066 and All That: A Memorable History of England*, intr. Frank Muir (Alan Sutton, 1993)

Shakespeare, William, *Macbeth: A Tragedy Acted at the Dukes-Theatre. London, Printed for William Cademan at the Popeshead in the New Exchange, in the Strand. 1673* (facsimile, Cornmarket Press, 1969)

Scheffler, Axel, *The Silent Beetle Eats the Seeds: Strange & Familiar Proverbs from Far and Wide* (Ted Smart, 1998)

Snowling, Margaret J. *Dyslexia* (Blackwell, 2000)

Strachey, Lytton, *Queen Victoria* (Chatto and Windus, 1921)

Vallins, G. H. *Spelling*, revised by D. G. Scragg (André Deutsch, 1965)

Walker, Janice R. and Todd Taylor, *The Columbia Guide to On-line Style* (Columbia University Press, 1988)

White, T. H. *The Goshawk* (Penguin, 1963)

Woolf, Virginia, *Travels with Virginia Woolf*, ed. Jan Morris (Pimlico, 1997)

Index